THE PHOENIX CODES

L. Sydney Fisher

MORE BY L. SYDNEY FISHER

STANDALONES
See No Evil
The Devil's Board

The Phoenix Series
The Phoenix Mission, Part I
The Phoenix Codes, Part II

The Bradford Series
The Haunting of Natalie Bradford, Part I
The Haunting of Natalie Bradford, Part II:
Waking the Dead
The Haunted Prophecy of Natalie Bradford:
The Complete Bradford Series

The Haunted Series
Volume I, The Devil's Den
Volume II, The Wilderness
Volume III, Possum Town
Volume IV, On the Haunted Trail

Dedicated with admiration and respect to the men and women of the United States Military. Past, present, and future.

To the men and women serving in any and all law enforcement agencies of federal, state, and local jurisdiction who protect our homeland.

I salute you.

And dedicated with love to ~

BRYCE, my star child

Editing provided by: Kathleen Hillman McCormick

PAPERBACK EDITION
ISBN-13: 978-1545089798
ISBN-10: 1545089795

Cover Design: L. Sydney Fisher

From the Author

Sergeant Major Seth Phoenix's story continues in *The Phoenix Codes* with the introduction of the HAARP program and the quest to duplicate his DNA codes. Although this story is fictional, there were times during my four years of research that I began to wonder if I was really writing fiction after all. The research was fascinating as I have spent a lifetime exploring the mysteries of psychic phenomena and paranormal activity.

Although the Star Gate program was officially shut down in November 1995 by the Clinton Administration, it is my opinion that the research may still be ongoing today under a black budget and an umbrella of secrecy, the truth about which we may never know.

To the men and women of our military, law enforcement, and all others who keep watch over the homeland, I salute you.

I hope that you enjoy the second book and the conclusion of this series.

L. Sydney Fisher

"People sleep peaceably in their beds at night only because rough men stand ready to do violence on their behalf."
– George Orwell

CHAPTER 1

A remote location somewhere near Fairbanks, Alaska, Sunday, November 12, 1995

As the Army Black Hawk helicopter landed, the force of its blades scattered snow across an open field surrounded by wilderness. Four Apache Attack helicopters flew in formation, surrounding the craft that transported America's soldiers and the most classified weapon in the world. As the Apache moved away and began circling the area, Sergeant Major Seth Phoenix shifted his 6'3" frame in his seat and stared out the side window of the aircraft. He was promised he wouldn't have to be here for long. Just a few weeks until any possibility of a media frenzy dies down. That would give the Clinton Administration and the CIA enough time to decide how to shut down Star Gate. Too many people were now aware of Seth Phoenix's existence, and four decades of paranormal studies were in danger of being exposed. Revealing the military's secret programs could lead to catastrophic vulnerability of the homeland.

Phoenix slowly placed one foot onto the ground, only to sink six inches deep into the frozen precipitation that now covered his feet up to his ankles. The wind blew a fine mist of icy snowflakes into his face, causing him to quickly squeeze his eyes shut. Two Army Rangers escorted him from the aircraft and motioned for Phoenix to follow them to a small, framed house less than 30 yards ahead.

The snow crunched loudly underneath the men's feet as they hurried to the front door. They stepped up and onto the porch. Phoenix stood aside as one of the rangers removed his right glove and pushed a ten-digit secret code into the lock securing the entrance. A small blue flash, followed by a single beep, signaled the men that the code had been accepted. The ranger pushed on the lock and opened the door.

Phoenix adjusted his military-issued sidearm, a Heckler and Koch .45, and glanced to the right and left of the ranger. He then followed him in and looked around at an empty room. The house was a shell with nothing inside to provide comfort. It was an illusion of constructed walls decorated from the outside in. The structure was designed to look like a little house in the woods, but it was a facade concealing an underground military shelter.

The two rangers moved quickly toward the center of the room. One of the men swept his foot across the floor, locating a hidden entry, while the other ranger quickly knelt and placed his palm and fingers flat against an invisible scanning pad. The ranger's identity was immediately recognized and recorded as a soft buzz sound. A low hum sounded as if a panel had opened in the floor, revealing a stairway and tunnel leading down to the secret bunker.

Phoenix knew the scene all too well, having spent weeks inside the bunker at Fort Meade. He started down the stairs. The two rangers followed close behind until they reached the door leading inside. Phoenix stepped up to the retina scan and leaned forward. The device hummed upon recognition, and the locks clicked open.

Phoenix turned and looked at the rangers, who gave him a thumbs-up, signaling the "okay" to enter, and at the same time, it was an indication that their part in Phoenix's transfer was ending. Phoenix nodded but hesitated for a moment before speaking.

"When will you be coming back for me?" Phoenix was comparing his notes to theirs and the time frame involved. He trusted no one.

Army Ranger Jason Garrett stared back at him. "Sergeant Major, weren't you briefed? We haven't received orders to return yet."

Phoenix studied Garrett's face. It had been at least three years since he had seen the man who had befriended him when the two of them were stationed at Fort Bragg. He had departed for Ranger training at Fort Benning, leaving Phoenix behind and uncertain of his role in the Army Special Forces division. That was then, but as Phoenix's piercing blue eyes stayed locked on his friend, he left no doubt in Garrett's mind that he wasn't trusting a damn soul.

The sergeant major nodded. "I was briefed." Then, without warning, Phoenix stepped forward and grabbed Garrett's arm. "I have no friends. Do you understand what I'm saying? I have no fucking friends right now. All I ask is that you don't let those bastards leave me here for months. I was told 'weeks'."

Garrett began shaking his head in exasperation. "We've got to go, Phoenix. The chopper is waiting. We've got to go." Phoenix read Garrett's eyes. He had been designated as the transport personnel but had wanted no part in the mission. He felt a twinge of regret.

Phoenix released his arm, and the ranger turned and ran toward the stairs leading to the outside. The chopper's blades, beating against the icy air, vibrated the metal banister as Garrett rushed to the top. He quickly climbed out and slammed the secret panel shut, locking it in place. Then he hurried to the door and across the snow, placing his feet back into the same set of footprints that he had just made minutes before. As he climbed into the chopper, he signaled the "all go" as the aircraft lifted off the ground.

Phoenix watched Garrett take his last step up the stairs leading to the outside. Then he turned and entered the door that led to an underground safe house. He was now in a 5,000-square-foot bunker with all the modern amenities he would need to survive. The underground pad was designed with a full kitchen, a laundry closet housing a dryer and a washing machine, a living room with a television, several bedrooms, dorm-like cubicles with bunk beds, and a full bathroom with a shower. The bunker also included at least five offices and conference facilities, as well as a small medical room stocked with a variety of first aid and surgical supplies.

Phoenix studied his surroundings and listened to the dead silence within the underground walls. He was now thousands of miles away from Washington, D. C., but was he as safe here as the doctor believed he would be? The United States government had been pushed into a corner. A corner that forced them to either preserve and protect Phoenix or kill him and erase any trace of his existence.

Phoenix walked into the living room and dropped his duffel bag to the floor. He eased down on the edge of the sofa and stared at the wall. As his eyes became fixed straight ahead, he began to feel a nauseating sensation and sharp, knife-like pains that radiated up the base of his neck and into his skull. He immediately recognized the pains that now served as a familiar reminder of the time when he was exposed to strong EMF waves. Exposure could cause severe sickness and interference with his supernatural abilities. He moved his head from side to side. He tried to shake the feeling and raked his fingers across the shaved remnants of his dark brown hair. But Phoenix had no idea that the bunker was located within a hundred miles of another secret military program headed by the U.S. Air Force and the U.S. Navy. And this secret program was much more sophisticated than the Star Gate operation at Fort Meade. Phoenix knew nothing about the electromagnetic fields that were pulsating dangerously close to his location. And he wasn't briefed on the proximity of his fiercest enemy either. Classified information had been withheld in a reckless attempt to control him. It had been two months since he had used clairvoyance. The last several weeks had been a welcome break from the energetic exhaustion that often followed his use of supernatural abilities, and he had not been given a reason to use them. Dr. O'Connor had convinced him that he would be protected, and Phoenix had believed him. Until now.

CHAPTER 2

*Inside The Oval Office at The White House
Sunday, November 12, 1995
4:33 p.m.*

President Bill Clinton greeted Dr. Nathaniel O'Connor and CIA Director John Deutch as the two men entered the Oval Office. Deutch closed the door behind him as the doctor walked to the front of the president's desk. In his hand, the director carried the final report and top-secret documents of the Star Gate project. The agency's final report included information deemed suitable for declassification. Twenty-plus years of highly classified research had been exposed beyond its perimeter. The special access program was operated in an underground world where fewer than 100 government officials were privy to its existence. Operated within the president's Black Budget, the CIA was now forced to shut down the operation or risk massive inquisitions from Congress and the public. Star Gate was the proof of psychic phenomena and remote viewing. If the research fell into the wrong hands, it could become the greatest threat to the country's security.

President Clinton stood up from his chair. Director John Mark Deutch locked eyes with the president as he handed him the declassified documents.

"The Star Gate headquarters has been relocated, Mr. President." The director waited as the Commander-in-Chief took the file.

"And Phoenix?" President Clinton flipped the file open and scanned the contents but didn't take the time to read anything in depth.

"Yes, he was transported early this morning to a classified location near Fairbanks."

"Fairbanks, Alaska?" The doctor's tone expressed surprise.

The director nodded and spoke to the doctor as he turned to look directly at him. "Yes, he was picked up at Eielson Air Force Base."

The doctor took a breath and studied the director's face. Deutch read his expression and knew that something wasn't settling well with him. He hesitated for a second, then spoke. "What is it?"

"I was just thinking--- The doctor rubbed his forehead with his fingers and paused.

"I was thinking about the proximity of Alaska to Russia. If the Russian girl---

The director looked confused as he interrupted. "We moved Phoenix to this location because it's extremely remote and only a handful of people know about it, but it's only about twenty miles from the base. If we need to get him out of there, we can do it faster than time travel, Doc."

The doctor nodded once and then asked. "Do you realize that this Russian woman can contact him if she chooses? She can penetrate his mind. See his location. The closer she is, the easier it will be. You just unlocked a door for her."

Director Deutch turned and looked at President Clinton. The president knew that he had to disclose further details about secret military programs unknown to the doctor. To protect America's most clandestine defensive weapon, known as Seth Phoenix, the doctor responsible for his health had to know about HAARP.

Deutch took a deep breath and motioned for the doctor to sit down in the chair next to him as he situated himself in front of the president's desk. The president took the director's invitation and returned to his seat as well.

"Dr. O'Connor, I need to make you aware---

Deutch took a breath and frowned, then continued. "About some information that has not been previously disclosed to you by me or anyone else at the CIA, as far as I know." The director paused.

The doctor looked at Deutch through squinted eyes. "Yes?" O'Connor's body stiffened as he traced his index finger across his upper lip.

"Two other branches of the military have been running a major research program for the last couple of years."

O'Connor's eyes widened as they locked in a near stare-down at the director. "What kind of research?"

Deutch shifted in his chair. "Similar research to the Star Gate program, but more focused on using and manipulating electromagnetic fields."

"I don't understand." The doctor cleared his throat.

"Doctor, the highly classified HAARP program is a research program jointly funded by both the United States Navy and Air Force. It's been summarized as a missile defense tool and a mind control device."

The doctor shook his head, indicating he needed more information. "Where is it?"

"It's located in Alaska near Phoenix's location." The director replied.

"Within 100 miles?" The doctor asked.

"Within 50 miles. And it's a very sophisticated system being used to test an electromagnetic pulse."

Dr. O'Connor wiped his hands across his forehead and down his face. He responded in a grave tone. "God damn it. I should have known about this before Phoenix was transported here."

The director leaned forward. "Why, Doctor?"

"These pulses act as a magnet with Phoenix's supernatural vibration. The electromagnetic pulses will consume him, depleting his powers. We've got to get him out of there right now." The doctor stood up.

"But we put him there because--- Deutch started to remind the Doctor of Security considerations, but he was interrupted by O'Connor's outburst.

"Jesus Christ, this could kill him!" The doctor shouted.

"John, wait a minute." The president raised his hand and motioned for Deutch to remain quiet. His tone was urgent and direct.

"Dr. O'Connor, we can get him moved, but I need to inform you about the significance of the research going on at HAARP. The program has been testing some of the same theories as the Star Gate program, but before we discovered the sergeant major, all of this was just lab work and hypothetical theories. We are at the forefront of mastering something beyond human comprehension, but we need to study Phoenix."

The doctor stared into the pale blue eyes of President Clinton, then searched his face as if he were expecting to uncover hidden messages.

The doctor felt his blood run cold. "Are you telling me that you transported Phoenix there to be studied?"

The president hesitated. "I'm telling you that the research being conducted within the walls of HAARP and the Stanford Institute is more sophisticated than anything you have done at Star Gate. And we have partners who are involved in stem cell research."

The doctor shook his head. "You mean cloning, don't you?"

The president looked at Deutch, then back at the doctor. "That's exactly what I mean. We need to study him, Dr. O'Connor. If Russia has the capabilities in Nikita Oleshun as we have in Phoenix, there's only one way to defend ourselves against them."

Chills crept over the doctor's body. "Duplicating his DNA?"

The president attempted to dissuade the doctor's concerns as he offered an explanation. "For the past three years, we've had more than a dozen scientists studying the phenomena that Seth Phoenix is able to generate at will."

A silent pause followed. The doctor covered his mouth with his hands and rested his chin in his palm. His eyes expressed doubt and certain fear at the thought of duplicating Phoenix's codes. Replicating them into an army of mindless human clones was the stuff horror movies were made of, and now the impossible was being considered in our race to stay ahead of advancements in Russian defense systems.

The doctor tapped his foot on the floor as he considered a response, but just as he opened his mouth, the director leaned forward like a lion cornering its prey. In a low and deep resounding tone, he confirmed the White House's intent. "We need his codes."

CHAPTER 3

Back at the secret bunker near Fairbanks, Alaska

The sergeant major massaged his temples and attempted to block out the interference that kept sweeping into his energy fields. He knew something wasn't right from the minute he exited the chopper. His skin began to tingle, and his stomach churned just as his feet hit the floor of the bunker. This was Alaska, and too close to Nikita Oleshun. *Didn't they know that?* Didn't they know that placing him on the cusp of Russia's front door would be the same as enabling Moscow's psychic spy with a telescopic sight that could probe Seth Phoenix any way she desired? The two of them had already proven that time and distance weren't barriers when tapping into their clairvoyant abilities but placing a top-secret psychic weapon along a back-door border just gave Russia an open channel.

Phoenix began to explore the other rooms in the bunker, finally making his way to a locked door that held secret answers to his sudden illness. He stopped outside the office and focused on the room inside. He felt weak and stumbled as he used his mental powers to enter the other side. If he attempted telekinesis to unlock the door, it could set off a hidden alarm.

Phoenix walked up close to the door and placed his hand on the doorknob. By touching the handle, he could tap into the energy of everyone who had entered the room and thereby access the information they held in their subconscious minds. His mind's eye showed him a cabinet with more locks, but he was able to penetrate the metal shell enclosing classified documents on a project he had never heard of. The front of a file folder was labeled HAARP.

Phoenix kept his eyes closed with his right index finger on his right temple and his left hand touching the door handle. Information flooded Seth's mind in a band of electrical waves. He struggled to mentally record important data as it raced across a railway of neurological connections. High Frequency Active Auroral Research Program. United States Navy and United States Air Force. Human Cloning. Mind Control. University of Alaska and the Defense Advanced Research Projects Agency. (DARPA)

Phoenix took a deep breath as he continued to mentally watch a mirage of research on a mental projector. He was stunned by the findings and unable to move, mesmerized by the discovery and the reality of the military's paranormal research programs. Star Gate was just the beginning, and in reality, it was hardly the central point of the research but rather an extension of an operation that was extending its roots into all branches of the military.

Phoenix hurriedly absorbed the data, but he took extra care to store bits of information related to paranormal remote-viewing studies. He made a mental effort to compartmentalize crucial data that might influence the government's interest in him. And as the pages of classified files flipped wildly in the recesses of his mind, the sergeant major stopped at once when his eyes met the secret files on human cloning.

Phoenix took time to read the first two papers in the file, making a mental note of the date printed in the top-right corner of page 1. *Were these the original documents printed and stored in this secret bunker deep in the Alaskan wilderness? And why?* Phoenix concluded that the documents he was reviewing were duplicates. These were duplicates of the original papers, bearing the wet signatures of the signatories. Papers that were now buried deep beneath the earth's surface.

Phoenix stood still, suspended in space and time as his fingers touched the projected image before him. November 5, 1995. That was just seven days ago. Phoenix scanned the paper and began reading aloud.

"University of Massachusetts scientists have successfully created a human clone using human cells implanted into a cow's ovum that had the genetic material removed. The human cells fused with the ovum and began dividing. Scientists (named in the official report) abandoned the project and destroyed the zygote when it reached the 32-cell stage. It is our educated hypothesis that the clone would develop into an identical twin of the human being whose retrieved cells were used in this experiment."

Phoenix sighed heavily and closed his eyes. A chill swept over him as he began mentally detaching himself from the viewing. He knew what was going on. He now knew why it was imperative that Star Gate be shut down and all traces of the program's existence be erased. And he knew the most significant reason for President Clinton's unrelenting need to protect him. He was about to become the government's most covert program ever. With the official operation now closed and the media silenced, the work could begin.

The sergeant backed away from the door and started to turn just as a surge of stabbing pain slammed against his face. As he fell backward, he flung his arms to the side and steadied himself against an invisible force that he wasn't prepared for. In the distance, HAARP was releasing electromagnetic pulses that had passed through the underground bunker's barriers and reached the sergeant. A normal person would most likely not be affected by the minute vibrations, but Phoenix was no average human being, and even the slightest change in electromagnetic fields could influence his tolerance of the unseen force and weaken his powers.

He felt a wave of pain and heard the vibrating hum as it pulsated in ripples before evaporating. His throat burned, and he began to cough and gag. His wrenching quickly caused him to vomit traces of bile from an otherwise empty stomach. As he bent over and grabbed his abdomen, he felt the warm, wet droplets of blood dripping into his hand. He examined his fingers and wiped his nose. As he touched the source of the blood's flow, his fingers became stained a bright, crimson red.

Phoenix was in trouble, and he was weakening fast. His supernatural powers became agitated as he now heard unknown voices. The sound of a woman's faint whisper repeated over and over. "Do not be afraid."

He slowly raised his head and began to put one foot in front of the other as he walked toward one of the nearby sleeping quarters. But just as he advanced a few feet into the hallway, he stopped dead still upon seeing the full body apparition of a woman he had seen once before.

Nikita Oleshun stood before Seth Phoenix in her teleported state. Although she was transparent, he could still easily look into the brunette's striking blue eyes that were just like his own. He froze, not wanting to put her on the defensive in his weakened state. He was vulnerable and didn't know whether he was a match for her if he had to defend himself against her power. She wasted no time and began delivering a message to him, spoken in English but with an unmistakable Russian accent.

"You mustn't tell anyone that I've been here. Your government is planning to use you by replicating your DNA codes. You mustn't allow this to happen. I am your exact match and a product of the Russian government's paranormal research programs. I have been under the control of the KGB for the last ten years. If your country successfully replicates our DNA, it will lead to the complete and utter annihilation of humankind. Do you understand?"

Phoenix's eyes widened as he listened to the faint, feminine voice of his supernatural mate. He stared at her in awe and disbelief. A distant childhood memory flashed through his mind, seeping in to comfort him and remind him of a time when he was safe.

Nikita Oleshun's voice began to trail away as the sergeant major's eyelids became heavy. He struggled to keep them open as he watched her, standing just ten feet away from him, now slumped against the wall. Then a loud and irritating ring burst forth and ended the dialogue as Phoenix's phone rang with an urgency that no doubt matched the circumstances. Phoenix reached into his right pocket and jerked the phone loose. He pushed the receiving button.

"Phoenix." He answered the phone in a low, gruff tone.

As he heard a familiar voice now loud and frantic from the other end, he watched the teleported apparition of Nikita Oleshun disappear right before his eyes.

"Sergeant Major, are you there?! Sergeant Major?!"

CHAPTER 4

The sergeant major immediately recognized the voice of his closest ally. The doctor was the last known person whom Phoenix believed he could trust in a world of powerful political agendas. As the doctor shouted into the phone, Seth fought against the dazed consciousness that kept forcing his eyelids closed. Phoenix's nasal cavity continued to drip warm droplets of blood that formed a canal as it dripped onto his lips and down his chin.

He then whispered into the phone. His speech was slow and slurred. "I'm here. What the hell is---? Get me out of here."

"Sergeant major, there's been a mistake. They sent you there — I didn't know, but I'm getting you out of there now. A chopper---it's coming. What--What is your condition?" The doctor was frantic. His words were clipped.

Seth took a deep breath. His eyes rolled from left to right as he looked around the room. "I feel like hell. My nose is bleeding, Man. Tell me. What the fuck is this?"

"There is a testing station near you. Electromagnetic fields. It's affecting you. I—

Seth interrupted. "HAARP."

The phone was silent for a moment. Dr. O'Connor realized that Phoenix now knew about the military program that had been in operation for at least two years, while Star Gate had been secretly operating out of Fort Meade. He hesitated to comment, unsure how Phoenix would react or whether he believed the doctor had no prior knowledge of the operation.

Phoenix spoke through lips now painted with blood. With his powers weakened, he was only able to pick up fragments of information from the doctor's mind across thousands of miles, but he was able to determine that the doctor was not aware of the program. "You didn't know about HAARP."

"I did not." The doctor relaxed and lowered his head as he spoke on the phone.

"Where are they taking me?" Phoenix asked.

A loud buzz penetrated the men's ears as the doctor began to speak. Static filled the airwaves, not allowing an audible passage of the doctor's response, but Phoenix was able to make out the faint sounds of the doctor's voice. And the words hit Phoenix like a sonic blast as he realized he might never escape.

"Homey Airport."

Phoenix dropped his head and mouthed the words, "Area 51".

Back at the Pentagon, CIA Headquarters

Director John Deutch sat across from President Clinton and Dr. O'Connor, who now listened intently as the Secretary of Defense, William Perry, delivered the latest horrifying intel from Bosnia.

"Mr. President, the Serbs have kidnapped a number of American soldiers during the last twenty-four hours. The last word we had was that they were being held for execution along with hundreds of Muslims already captured."

The electricity in the room intensified as the men shifted in their seats. "Do you know their location and condition?" The president leaned forward.

"Air surveillance hasn't been reliable because of the hostility in the region, but the last ground intel we have indicates they're beat up like hell. Location is an abandoned school building near Srebrenica."

"How the hell did this happen?" Deutch mouthed under his breath.

"We believe the attack on American peacekeepers came at 0300 hours. They were completely caught off guard. It's not safe for a ground rescue mission. The Serbs are firing rockets and heavy artillery, repelling any attempt to enter the area."

Dr. O'Connor traced his lips with his fingers and turned to look at the president. He said one word. "Phoenix."

All eyes turned to the doctor as the Secretary of Defense, Perry, asked, "Where is he now?"

The doctor made eye contact with the secretary. "He's in Fairbanks awaiting transport to Homey."

The secretary leaned back in his chair and shook his head. "We need him. Get him back at Fort Meade and get him ready to go to Bosnia. The only way we're going to get in there to rescue our troops before those bastards behead them is by some supernatural force. And Phoenix is it."

The doctor and the CIA Director glanced back at President Clinton as they waited for his response. Dr. O'Connor spoke. "Mr. President?"

Clinton nodded, then held his finger up and pointed to Perry. "You instruct the military that Phoenix is to be protected at all costs. We cannot lose him. We've got too much at stake." Clinton's tone was forceful and direct. Phoenix had become his own prized possession in the race to beat Russia's advances in military science. Although Phoenix and his abilities could never become public knowledge, he could pave the way for future warfare. A supernatural soldier designed by duplicating DNA.

The men started to push their chairs back from the table when the doctor halted them. His tone was urgent.

"Wait a minute. I just spoke with Phoenix a couple of hours ago. He knows about HAARP, and the electromagnetic pulses in the area are beating the hell out of him."

Clinton was silent for a moment before he turned his attention to the Secretary of Defense.

"Secretary Perry, forget about taking him to Homey. Dr. O'Connor will meet Phoenix at Fort Meade." The president turned to the doctor.

"Doctor, I need you there when that chopper lands."

"Time is running out. He needs to be ready to go in 24 hours." Secretary Perry added. The urgency in his tone was evident.

The doctor nodded. "Yes, Mr. President, of course." He pushed his chair back and turned to leave the room. He opened the door and walked out. As it closed behind him, Deutch leaned over and whispered to the Defense Secretary.

"Does he know about the research at Stanford?"

Perry shrugged his shoulders. "I'm unaware if he does or not, but when the mission is complete, he'll know. And Phoenix *will* cooperate."

"And if he doesn't?" Deutch questioned.

The president stood silent along with Perry. Both men hesitated to answer the question that both of them already knew the answer to. If Phoenix refused orders from the United States Pentagon, he could find himself walking into a landmine of his own making.

CHAPTER 5

Hours later, near Srebrenica, Bosnia

The chopper's blinking red and white taillights were barely visible against a cloudy night sky as an Army ranger prepared to assist Phoenix out of the chopper. The sergeant major positioned himself for the fast-roping maneuver and grabbed onto the rope as he swung himself outward while securing his feet. He moved swiftly and used his gloved hands to steady himself on the rope as he lowered his body. His movement was lightning-fast, like a fireman sliding down a pole, while heat-resistant gloves shielded his hands from the burning sting of the descent. In less than fifteen seconds, Phoenix was on the ground.

His feet were almost silent as they tapped the thick grassy earth. His stealth and agile movement were much like a lion's prowess as the sergeant major now found himself in the same mountain territory where American soldiers had just been captured and taken hostage hours before. Time was not an ally, and Phoenix knew that his assault had to be swift and paralyzing lest he lose the lives that he came to save.

A team of deadly special forces joined him as they exited their hidden posts shielded under a canopy of trees. Several members of the unit were American allies from the U.N., but the peacekeepers had not been successful in driving the Serbs out of the area as the invasion reached critical proportions. Mass graves were scattered across the landscape, housing the innocent bodies of thousands of men and boys who had died just weeks before from genocide or execution.

Phoenix looked into the masked faces of his team as the men huddled together. He quickly delivered instructions and then motioned for the men to move out. The team would have to provide a secure outside parameter as the hostages were being freed and guided through the main street toward the armored vehicles that would be waiting. Phoenix would be on his own once he was inside the walls of the abandoned town, now densely populated with starving citizens.

Phoenix wasted no time in his departure as he rushed down the hillside leading to the edge of the town. The building that reportedly held the hostages was located just yards from his entry point at the bottom of a deep slope. Phoenix's boots seemed to lift off the ground as he moved with precision. As he neared the outermost wall, he detected conversation coming from the other side. He squatted to the ground, then quickly found cover behind a thick band of trees where he sat down and waited a few moments. He homed in on the chatter coming from the hostage point. *Changing guards.*

Phoenix slowly peeked from behind the tree and focused his eyes straight ahead. Through the thick brush, he could see the town's lights and the statues of people walking in and out of the building that he was about to storm. He cleared his mind of all other interference until he was almost in a trance-like state. He watched and assessed the movements of the Serbs before him. Even the sounds of the creatures of the night faded as if they had never existed as the sergeant major prepared for the danger before him. Then he stepped from behind the trees, his eyes fixed on the target straight ahead. With stealth and precision, he made his final descent down the hillside and into enemy territory.

As Sergeant Major Seth Phoenix approached, the danger and complexity of the mission intensified as several Serbs began pacing in front of the building. *Had someone tipped them off?* Phoenix planted his feet firmly behind a cluster of shrubs, barely hidden from sight. He sent a magnetic blast to the Serbian soldiers that pierced their ears. Three Serbians fell screaming to their knees as blood poured out from busted eardrums.

Phoenix then ran for it, bolting forward. His blue eyes glowed against the dark night as he hurried past the fallen men. His body temperature was rising along with the intensity of his heart rate; He knew that the supernatural power he would need to access could cause fatigue and get him killed. But just as Phoenix turned the corner, he met more Serbs now responding to the screams of the fallen men.

Phoenix's finger rested on the trigger until that moment when hesitation was his biggest enemy. He fired off several rounds from the M4 strapped across his shoulder, the bullets pummeling into the thoracic cavities of three captors. Phoenix breathed fast and heavy as he dodged rounds that spewed from a dead man's gun. His lifeless fingers were lodged in the trigger pull of his weapon, and it had been his last and final attempt to kill the sergeant major.

Phoenix caught a split second of relief as he leaned against the outside wall. His eyes darted all around him, and his ears listened to the sounds of someone's whispers from inside the building. *English speaking. American soldiers.*

He heard the racing thumps of the Serbs' boots against the hard ground as dozens of them rushed from opposite sides of the building. Phoenix jerked his arms into the air with rocket speed, raising them with palms facing out as his body sent waves of electromagnetic energy toward the band of Serbs now determined to kill him. The mega-force of energy slammed into them, one by one, causing them to fall like dead flies. The popping sound of their ribs snapping like thin tree branches burned into Phoenix's ears as the sound of their screams followed the excruciating pain.

Phoenix maintained his position until he heard the radio signal from the outside team telling him to "launch", indicating that time was up, and he had to move now. As Phoenix's supernatural adrenaline flowed fast and hard through his veins, he orchestrated the top-secret rescue operation in split seconds. He felt an euphoric sensation as his feet seemed to lift off the ground, carrying him toward a blocked door that led into the hostage holding cell.

Phoenix raised his hand and slammed a bolt of energy against the barricade, sending it off its hinges. He then stormed through the splintered wood fragments and scanned the room with the agile skill known only to the best of the best in special ops training.

Wide eyes stared back at him in disbelief and horror as dozens of emaciated men and boys lay huddled together near the center of the room. The starving captives stumbled to their feet and scurried toward Phoenix, who motioned for them to exit the building. Fear covered their bearded faces, hiding the glimmer of hope that they had held onto for the past two weeks. As the last hostage passed out the door, the special ops team directed them to the caravan hidden by the night sky and waiting only yards away.

Phoenix looked perplexed as he viewed a now-empty room that was believed to hold American soldiers. *Where the hell were they?* He quickly adjusted his radio and clicked the button to speak but hesitated just as he heard mental chatter zooming into his mind. The pupils of Phoenix's eyes swelled as he began to receive visual information. Then an unexpected thud came hard against a makeshift door near the back wall beneath his feet. He sprinted across the floor and slid to the ground as he swept his hands across a wooden panel bolted to the floor. Mental images flashed before him as he visualized the interior of a manmade hole where the beaten and battered American Joes had been dumped.

The sergeant major breathed heavily before he spoke into the mic and notified the team that he needed help.

"Defender 1, this is Falcon. The nest is not empty." Phoenix's voice was clear, his words quick and clipped.

"Roger that, Falcon. Did you find Joe?"

"Affirmative, all of them are underground. Need assistance, over."

"Roger that. Stand by."

Phoenix then stood two feet away from the panel door and raised his hands with his palms facing down and directly in front of him as he prepared to send a blast of energy strong enough to crumble the metal locks. Sweat was now dripping from his eyebrows as Phoenix radiated a force aimed at the floor. The soldiers inside the hole covered their heads as they felt the loud boom vibrate the pit.

Phoenix reacted with a rapid fury as he bent down and wiped his hands across the locks, literally slinging the charred metal fragments across the room. He placed his fingers in a firm hold around the broken handle and pulled back with an unyielding force as he hurled the door into the air, sending it flying to the right of him and into the wall.

Just as Phoenix looked down into the pit, he sensed Special Ops Team Members, Defender One, and Raptor Three approaching from behind. He jerked around and made first contact as he signaled for them to join his location. With lightning speed, the men dropped their gear and lowered a rope into the pit as Raptor Three latched on and slid down into the hole. He spoke softly, giving the soldiers instructions as he assisted them in forming a human pyramid. As the men were thrust upward within arm's reach, Phoenix latched onto each one, raising each soldier out of the hole with astral force.

Seconds seemed like hours as Phoenix whispered the words, "Go, go, go!" Raptor Three zipped up the rope being held by Phoenix and Defender One. But just as the men turned to race out of the building, the terrifying, familiar sound filled their ears as they heard the repeated clink and thump of IED bombs being thrown through a window.

"Get out, get out now!" Phoenix yelled.

Defender One followed Raptor Three as the two men exited the entry point, and the rest of the team followed in retreat.

Time seemed to slow down as the sergeant major became disoriented. He had reached his body's peak energy expulsion and was about to lose consciousness as the last IED flew through the window, landing inches away from his feet. Phoenix shook his head and struggled to scramble toward the exit point. His body temperature was now dangerously high as he fought the urge to close his eyes. As his feet landed outside the front entry, Phoenix fell to one knee. A bomb detonated, releasing an ear-splitting boom, and the total desolation of the building's north wall crumbled before him. Shards of debris blasted Phoenix, slicing open his left brow as blood saturated the outer rim of his helmet. Then, without warning, he felt a swift and superhuman force grab him by the back of his jacket and lift him completely off his feet while dragging him away with a metaphysical speed only known by his own strength.

Phoenix's feet barely touched the grass as his rescuer raced away from the area, moving him up the hillside as he attempted to tune into the movements of Defender One and Raptor Three. He knew they had made it out of the building before the explosion, but it was no use. Just as he attempted to focus, he was dropped to the ground with a thud as the unknown hero, dressed in camouflage and now barely visible, stood over him, radio in hand. As Phoenix pried his eyes open, he stared in astonishment as he studied the figure standing before him, whose true identity remained unknown. The masked agent watched Phoenix and stepped away before offering an introduction.

The secret agent began peeling away the face gear that hid the agent's identity. As the mask was lifted away from the chin, Phoenix observed the faint outline of a smug smile followed by a voice he had heard before.

"Sergeant Major Phoenix, we meet again."

CHAPTER 6

Sergeant Major Seth Phoenix coughed and blinked multiple times as he stared into the pale blue eyes of the Russian spy. For the first time, he was viewing Nikita Oleshun in the present, standing before him, not a teleported hologram. That only meant that her strength had to be magnified thousands of times more than he had experienced months ago when the two of them had met at the Kremlin in an astral mission that threatened to kill him. And now he found himself vulnerable again to a supernatural human the world knew nothing about.

Phoenix studied her. Could she read his thoughts? Or was her power only limited to telekinesis? Before he had a chance to ponder the questions, she interrupted his mental dialogue.

"Yes, Sergeant Major—or can I just call you Phoenix?" Her Russian accent was heavy and her voice low, yet sultry.

Phoenix hesitated to answer and decided to remain silent for a moment longer as he continued to search the Russian's eyes. He was weak and not fully capable of delivering a massive telekinetic assault against her. Not one that he could win anyway, but his mental impulses were still useful in stealing information directly from the frontal lobe of another's brain before the words even had a chance of escaping their lips.

Nikita Oleshun was a dangerous, yet stunning beauty. Although her body was well covered by the armor and military attire that she wore, the image of her face carved an imprint in Phoenix's mind that would be difficult to forget. She had just saved his life and had become an ally at that moment when she lifted the 210-pound man off his feet and delivered him to safety. As he attempted to process the reality of the Russian's heroic act, he began to take mental snapshots of her features. Her piercing, almond-shaped blue eyes were defined by the perfect oval shape of her face. And her smooth, olive complexion complemented the dark brown twigs of hair that lay disheveled and strewn about her head.

"I should thank you for getting me out of there," Phoenix said as he leaned forward and started to stand. He decided to test the waters with friendly banter. It was worth the risk since she could read his thoughts anyway, and he could steal a moment longer until he decided what the hell he needed to do next.

Nikita nodded but didn't have time to waste. She then motioned for him to wait as she placed her hand out in front of her. "Before we move out—

Phoenix interrupted. "What do you want from me?"

Nikita took a breath. "My government will be looking for me in a few minutes. I have to radio in, or they'll come for me."

Phoenix's gaze became a hard stare as he zeroed in on her, invading her mind but wasting no more time and tossing the friendly maneuver out the window as he demanded answers.

"We can play this mind-reading shit another time, but right now, you need to tell me what the fuck is going on and why you just saved my ass."

Nikita ignored him and quickly jerked her face gear back in place. She motioned for Phoenix to follow as she sprinted forward, making her way deeper into the trees. The commotion from the IED blasts still lingered at the foot of the hill but was fast becoming a distant echo as she and Phoenix now moved out of the area with rapid speed. The night vision gear she wore aided in locating a cave where she had hidden out just moments before Phoenix's rescue mission commenced. She carefully stepped across a rocky path as Phoenix followed. He stumbled behind her but quickly gained his footing as the two entered the mouth of the cave. Just as Nikita made it safely out of sight, she rested against the inner wall and jerked the headgear off.

"My team thinks I'm dead. I have to report— Phoenix stated in a commanding tone. He breathed heavily and wiped his forehead.

"Listen to me. We have no more time." Nikita urged, her eyes darting all around as if she believed they were being followed.

"No, I have to- Phoenix argued.

"Just shut up. Shut up now! You can read minds, but you don't know when to shut up." Nikita blasted Phoenix through gritted teeth. The sergeant major stayed quiet, waiting for her to continue, and looking at her as if she had just lost her damn mind. He reached inside his pants pockets and pulled out a handful of high-protein rations. He quickly ripped open the wrappers and devoured them before emptying a canteen of water that Nikita handed him as he swallowed his last bite.

"I was sent here to gather information about you and obtain a sample of your DNA. We—I mean, the Russian government has been watching you since you were exposed weeks ago at the Kremlin. I am a servant to the KGB, now known as the SVR, Foreign Intelligence Service. I am a prisoner of my government because of my abilities, but until you surfaced, I was the only known human of my kind. We believe that your government is also planning to use you. Do you understand?"

Phoenix began to sweat. Every cell in his body simultaneously seemed to come alive, and his skin began to tingle as dread swept over him. "Use me?" He knew what for, but he wanted Nikita to confirm his suspicions.

"Sergeant Major, Russia and America are at war to see who'll be first to replicate the DNA of a superhuman."

Phoenix rested his forearm against his head and wiped away particles of sand and dirt that stuck to his skin during the explosion. He sighed heavily as he spoke. "They're planning to engineer a damn supernatural army."

"That is correct. You were transported to Alaska for research. I've been in your head for weeks."

Phoenix frowned and glanced at Nikita with one eyebrow cocked. "But Alaska didn't work out as planned."

Nikita nodded. "HAARP. The U.S. Navy and Air Force have been partners in the program since 1993."

"Electromagnetic field testing for controlling the weather?" Phoenix inquired but knew the Russian probably already knew more than he did.

Nikita laughed, then replied in her heavy Russian accent, her words pronounced in a mocking tone. "Is that what they say?"

Phoenix huffed and forced a half-cocked smile, but he was feeling more overwhelmed by the second. "No, mind control."

"What now? We can't stay here." Phoenix's tone changed abruptly as he demanded to know Nikita Oleshun's next move.

"The Kremlin is tracking me. I have to report what happened back there."

"That mission was highly classified. No one knew about it." Phoenix stated. He instantly realized the magnitude of Nikita Oleshun's breach.

"As I said, I've been with you. When I realized what our governments were doing, I knew I could no longer remain loyal to the country that I loved and served for all these years. They have become something else. Something that threatens civilization as we know it."

Her voice trailed off at the end of her last sentence. At once, the Russian spy remembered a time from her past, an easier life ten years before, when she was in love and free from the constraints of her powers. As a sergeant in the Russian military, Nikita had become the country's most guarded and clandestine citizen.

Like Phoenix, Nikita's supernatural powers were discovered during a deadly battle that sent her directly into an artillery barrage. The attack happened ten years before, while Nikita and her fiancé were serving in Kabul. Because military romance was frowned upon, the two Russian soldiers had loved each other in secret. Their love had gone unknown until then, but they had high hopes of leaving the Russian army and starting a life together.

That fatal moment ensued as a blazing projectile of bullets filled the air, exploding dozens of metal cartridges in every direction as she fought to save Sergei's life. Nikita sent an electromagnetic force forward, crushing the assailant's heart as his sternum split in half from the impact. Blood spurted from his mouth as he fell to the ground, but it was too late for Sergei, who had taken a shot that severed his jugular.

Nikita Oleshun wailed as she stood over the body of the man who was to be her husband. Her knees buckled from under her, and she fell by his side as she lifted him into her arms. She kissed his eyelids and brushed her lips against his while mumbling "I love you" between gut-wrenching sobs. The horrific event was now a distant memory, but she still felt a sting of pain each time she remembered the warmth of his love and the emptiness she had felt without it for the past ten years.

Nikita shook herself back to reality and stared back into the eyes of a man whose physical traits resembled those of the man and the memory she cherished. There had been no one else who had come close to filling her heart since Sergei's death, and yet she inwardly begged to be relieved from his memory's grip. Lonely had become her middle name.

Phoenix's eyes blinked in response to Nikita's confession. At that moment, he felt one with her. He now knew her story and how the two of them had come to this place. It was as if destiny had led them here, and there was no other explanation for it. Phoenix had not known a woman's real love in years. Cursed by his own belief that no one would ever accept his strangeness, he had never married and had been alone for the past couple of years, other than the few meaningless, short-lived romances that he had entertained. It had ultimately left him unfulfilled and emptier than ever, but he had no remedy for his anguish. No solution or fix. And so, he maintained the familial relationships that had proven tried and true throughout his life back in Chattanooga. It was his safe place.

Now Nikita Oleshun stood before him, her soul naked and undone. At that moment, he realized that he had a friend and an equal but staying with her meant certain death to them both.

"I have to go." Phoenix forced the words out of his mouth.

Nikita stared into Phoenix's eyes, which appeared pained and soulful as he looked at her. She felt his vibration and knew that he would no longer be a threat to her. "Phoenix?"

The sergeant major sensed what she was about to ask. He placed his hand in hers, giving it a soft squeeze, and answered before the words left her lips. "I will."

Nikita then stated the secret landline numbers aloud.

"01174951230001."

Just then and without warning, Nikita's radio began to buzz. A voice broke through the static with an urgent call to the Russian spy now guilty of treason. She flinched and placed her finger on the receiver as Seth Phoenix turned and disappeared into the dark.

CHAPTER 7

The special ops commander, Defender One, repeatedly sought contact with Phoenix while shouting into the radio mic. The sergeant major could now hear the static of radio traffic as the commander's voice bled in and out in a maddening attempt to reach him, but Phoenix hesitated to answer. Although he knew he had to escape the area, he also realized that he had to think fast. He had just been rescued by Russia's coveted agent, and she was now in danger of being charged with a crime punishable by death if the Russians discovered her betrayal.

The soles of Phoenix's feet were hot, and his legs ached from the high speed of his retreat as he left Nikita Oleshun behind. He slowed his pace until he reached a stopping point near the site where the chopper had first dropped him. He bent over and rested his hands on his knees as he listened to fragments of noise up to a mile away. He breathed deep, relaxing his body from the sudden spike of energy he had managed to regain. The sound of the helicopter's blades chopped through the night air as Phoenix zeroed in and assessed the distance of the bird that would be landing within minutes.

Phoenix had to make a quick determination about the Russian soldier-turned-spy. If he failed to disclose his encounter with her, he could be arrested, but if the plot was as deep as she disclosed, his life and the future life of mankind might be at stake. Duplicating the DNA of Seth Phoenix and Nikita Oleshun could have cataclysmic consequences, but the two most powerful governments on the planet were now arranging plans to use both of the superhumans as lab specimens. He had to maintain a stance of ignorance for the moment. Just until he reaches the homeland. He had to return to Fort Meade in spite of the White House's determination to place him at Homey Airport.

Phoenix spotted the chopper's location as he continued north. He halted for a second and held his breath as he focused on the narrow path before him. The bird was there to pick him up, and he could no longer ignore the loud radio signals now coming through. He had to answer. How would he account for the loss of time since escaping the explosion? He would have to hope no one asked any questions. At this point, no one had any reason to be suspicious, but Phoenix simply could not divulge the details of what had just occurred with Nikita Oleshun.

Phoenix reached down and placed his finger on the receiver button. He applied a crushing force to the device, disabling it from sending communications. Nobody on the special ops team needed to know that she had even been there. He knew if he disclosed her identity or location to anyone, he would be risking her life and possibly his own. Although the government had promised the sergeant major uncompromising support and cover, he knew there was no one whom he could trust. Dr. Nathaniel O'Connor had pledged to safeguard the sergeant major, but Phoenix knew that the doctor's efforts would be thwarted if the big shots at the CIA decided he was a threat.

Phoenix's mind reeled as he processed information and scenarios through his mind. He broke into a fast run as soon as he moved into a clearing where he was now visible to the men loading the chopper. Defender One immediately noticed the sergeant major and ran to meet him. He shouted, but his voice was muffled by the loud thunder of the chopper's blades.

Phoenix read the commander's lips and nodded as he rushed to the side opening. He quickly placed one foot on the landing and hoisted himself in as Defender One followed.

Phoenix buckled the seatbelt and leaned back, resting his head on the back of the seat. The crew that had just escaped the IED seconds before it detonated now sat before him with questioning eyes. The sergeant major refrained from engaging in any banter as he attempted to relax his body, but a sudden and unanticipated surge of information crossed his mind, causing a sense of dread.

As the chopper began to lift off the ground, Phoenix became anxious. He grabbed his seat buckle and yanked at the belt, slinging it to the side just as the crew chief and the co-pilot glanced over at Phoenix as he was moving out of his seat.

"Sergeant Major, what are you doing?" The crew chief motioned for Phoenix to stop.

Phoenix ignored him and moved closer, positioning himself behind the pilot's seat. "Major, where are you taking me?"

Phoenix knew before he answered. The pilot glanced around. "Don't you know?"

Phoenix remained quiet, his eyes locked on the crew chief sitting beside him.

"You'll be departing for home the same way that you arrived." The pilot confirmed.

At that moment, Phoenix realized that the messages he was picking up on were coming straight from the Pentagon. He was being rerouted to Homey Airport after landing at Fort Meade. The sergeant major calmed down and eased back into his seat. He had to get off that plane and contact the doctor. He felt a sigh of relief for a brief moment until he overheard a startling statement from the cockpit.

"We have orders to transport Phoenix to Homey after we reach the homeland. He is not to leave our command."

Phoenix jumped forward, returning to the same position behind the pilot's seat. He gave the crew chief a warning stare as the crew chief reached to unfasten his seatbelt. Then Phoenix spoke in a loud, indisputable tone.

"Sergeant, I don't give a fuck what your orders are or who the fuck they came from. I'm getting off that plane when it reaches Fort Meade."

CHAPTER 8

Back at The Pentagon

The sound of the doctor's footsteps echoed through the halls of The Pentagon as he walked briskly toward Director Deutch's office. He knew that Phoenix would be returning to Fort Meade. The commander had already radioed central command about the explosion before Phoenix ever made it to the chopper. The doctor knew about the final orders. Phoenix would be hidden underground at Area 51, under the control of the U.S. government and the world's highest level of military security. If someone wanted Phoenix dead or planned to kidnap him, it would be impossible.

The doctor reached Deutch's office and knocked on the door. He heard the director's voice as the door opened from the inside. As O'Connor entered the room, he scanned the faces of the men and wondered which ones were behind the DNA operation designed to duplicate Phoenix's codes. The doctor walked around the table and took a seat across from the director. The director immediately addressed the doctor as he sat down.

"Phoenix barely escaped alive." The director maintained a calm tone.

Dr. O'Connor's eyes widened. "What happened?"

"Central Command informed us that Phoenix was caught inside after the rest of the hostages cleared. Serbians then stormed the building with IED's. Phoenix miraculously made it out just as they detonated, but---

"He's en route here? I want to see him." The doctor interrupted."

"Yes, the plane will land here, but the crew has orders to immediately transport Phoenix to Homey."

The doctor shook his head. "I need to see him. You know that I've been at the forefront of this research and this program since the beginning. I need to evaluate his condition."

The director hesitated, then continued. "We don't think that's a good idea, doctor."

"What? What are you talking about?" The doctor never cared much for Deutch and considered him a sneaky bastard.

The director turned and looked at the president, then back at the doctor. "We think Phoenix was *rescued*." The director emphasized his last word.

"Rescued?"

"Yes, rescued. Phoenix was the last known person inside that building when it blew. And it was loaded to hell and back with explosives. The rest of the team watched the inferno from the trees. Phoenix was nowhere to be found. Until---

"What the hell are you saying? Why did you send Phoenix to Bosnia? The sergeant major doesn't need to be rescued. He's capable—

The director nodded and held up his index finger. "Yes, but intel informed us yesterday that Russia had deployed troops to Srebrenica. We believe one of those soldiers was Nikita Oleshun."

The doctor slowly leaned forward. "What the hell is going on? Nikita Oleshun is-- "

Deutch interrupted, forcing the doctor to listen. "That is correct, Doctor. We now have intel that confirms Russia's DNA research. If the Russians succeed, they will be the first superpower capable of producing a soldier like their own Nikita Oleshun."

"My God. How long has this been going on?"

The director took a breath. "Years, maybe. But we believe Nikita Oleshun was in Srebrenica during this operation." The director tapped the table.

Dr. O'Connor traced his index finger across his lips as he considered the possibility that Oleshun had helped Phoenix escape. If she had helped the sergeant major or given him any information, she could have been charged with treason by the Russian government.

"We cannot pursue this research on Phoenix. We cannot be a part of something of this magnitude. This idea of duplicating Phoenix's DNA to reproduce superhuman soldiers. It's unethical. This soldier—the sergeant major---he's a man, not a damn robot."

No one spoke as the doctor continued. "Gentlemen, we've been cloning since 1952, when the first tadpole was cloned. But that doesn't make this research appropriate for humans. To hell with your agendas. To hell with the research. This is a treacherous attempt at world domination, and I'm going to tell you --- and."

The doctor paused and looked into the faces of the men now listening to him through narrowed eyes. Dr. O'Connor realized he was alone at that moment. He was stating an opposition that no one else in the room supported. As the doctor absorbed the coldness of their stares, he issued a final and fateful warning on the sergeant major's behalf.

"Phoenix will never agree to let you do this. He'll never agree to give you what you want. If you try to force the sergeant major into this, you'll be opening a Pandora's box. He has killed before, Gentlemen. We trained him to recognize the enemy. You'd better be certain that he doesn't mistake you for one."

Director Deutch shifted in his chair as the president turned to the doctor.

"What time is that plane due at Meade?" The president asked and looked back at Deutch.

The director was consumed with the reality of the consequences before him. After a long pause, he mumbled aloud and glanced in the doctor's direction. "Nine hours. He'll be there in nine hours."

CHAPTER 9

MOSCOW, The Kremlin

Nikita Oleshun adjusted her sidearm and unfastened the seatbelt strapped across her legs as the Russian Mil Mi-24 helicopter gunship, otherwise known as "Crocodile," landed outside the Kremlin. As she stood up and moved toward the side door, she felt a pair of powerful eyes watching her as she exited. She placed her hand on the side of the door and quickly searched the perimeter of people now gathering on the landing pad. Just as she scanned the rear left of the chopper, she locked eyes with Prime Minister Vladimir Putin, who maintained a poker face.

Nikita sensed impending danger and, without further hesitation, began accessing Putin's thoughts. She deliberately looked away from the prime minister and stepped out of the attack helicopter, placing one foot at a time on the side-step ladder leading to the ground. As Nikita sent invisible currents across the distance, penetrating Putin's mind, she caught herself just as she was about to gasp aloud. *He knew she was there*. Inside his mind. And he was playing it to his advantage, leading the Russian spy into a Machiavellian territory she wasn't prepared for.

Putin sent a signal aimed at Nikita Oleshun. He intended for her to see the images that he was producing in his mind. Images of her participation in the Kremlin-backed research for human cloning. The Russians had already produced the first psychic spy in the world, and they would be the first to produce multiples of her offspring. Genetically engineered to lead the race to become the most powerful country on the planet.

Nikita's blood ran cold the moment she looked into his mind. Although Putin was intentionally juggling his thoughts like a recorder repeatedly rewinding its data, she was able to hear the prime minister's future conversation, and she managed to slice through the veil of deception. He was there to escort her directly to President Yeltsin, who was waiting along with members of the Foreign Intelligence Service. She was about to give her debriefing of the Americans' mission in Srebrenica. And the Kremlin already knew she had been there.

Nikita had to make a quick decision about how to assume an apathetic posture toward Phoenix. *Could she disguise herself from the government that had taught her the ways of being a spy?* She had to. She had no choice. If she exposed herself now, they would kill her. She was certain of it. She had to convince them that Phoenix was dead.

Putin spoke to Nikita and motioned for her to enter the SUV. As she stepped forward, the prime minister lightly brushed against her forearm. A surge of images flashed before her, sending her into a dizzy spin as she struggled to maintain her balance. Nikita quickly fought off the urge to vomit and climbed into the vehicle. As she sat down and leaned back against the seat, her lips moved in a silent affirmation. *There is no other way out now.*

Fort Meade, Maryland
Department of Homeland Security
1500 hours

The sound of Deutch's shoes on the pristine, polished floor of the Department of Homeland Security could be heard as he approached the classified area reserved for top-secret meetings. Phoenix was just seconds behind the unsuspecting director, pushing past anything and anyone in his way as he neared Hall C. Dr. O'Connor was inside waiting. The doctor was prepared for his arrival. He had a medical kit in hand and three lunch trays that he had ordered to be delivered as soon as he got word that the chopper had landed on the base. By the time the sergeant major arrived, the food would be ready and delivered from the campus cafeteria.

O'Connor knew how detrimental it was for Phoenix to be fully replenished after enduring an episode of telekinesis. The depletion of energy could take days to recover if he was not fully restored by nutrition and intravenous fluids. The supernatural gift came with a high-maintenance price.

Phoenix passed the retina scan and slammed his forearm against the door as he made a hard entry into the room. Deutch froze as he observed the sergeant major standing before him. Phoenix was dirty and greasy, his hair disheveled, and his hands covered with scrapes and scratches from the shards of debris that blasted forth from the explosion. His body ached now, and he needed food. Lots of it. Although he was gravely weakened, his present state served as a warning to the doctor who knew his capabilities and the severity of consequences that could develop if Phoenix wasn't able to control his impulses.

"Sergeant Major." The doctor jumped to his feet as he spoke.

Phoenix stopped just inside the door.

The doctor motioned for Phoenix to sit. The sergeant major paused, searching the eyes of the men before collapsing into a rolling chair seated in front of the doctor. Phoenix stared at Dr. O'Connor through bloodshot eyes.

"Doc, get me-- Phoenix's speech became slurred as he was overcome with a need for sleep. He slumped forward and then, without warning, Phoenix jerked upright. The table began to vibrate, and the men stared in shock and awe.

The doctor wasted no time and quickly jumped around the table to Phoenix's side as he opened his medical bag and administered an injection of Valium. The injection immediately calmed his muscle reactions and slowed his heart rate and breathing. Because Phoenix couldn't control his bodily impulses during periods of severe depletion, it was imperative that he slow his metabolism and begin metabolic restoration. Although its effects on his central nervous system were short-lived, the drug worked remarkably well with his body's natural chemicals to produce a calming effect.

A tap on the door signaled that Phoenix's food had arrived. Deutch opened the door as an unknown government worker placed the trays on the table in front of Phoenix, then turned and left with the same urgency that he had exhibited upon delivering the food.

"Dr. O'Connor, this man needs medical attention. We can't send him out of here through the front. God damn reporters are swarming the front entrance. Take him underground after he eats." Deutch ordered.

"Yes, of course." Dr. O'Connor watched Phoenix, making sure he didn't collapse again.

Phoenix rolled his eyes to the side and studied the director. He slowly sat up in the chair and pulled three trays loaded with a variety of meats toward him. The famished soldier picked up a fork and began shoveling chunks of chicken, fish, and beef into his mouth, savoring each bite. His headache and mind fog began to dissipate as his body refueled and returned to a stable condition. Although he was still under the influence of the Valium injection, the drug's potency would not linger long.

"Mr. Deutch, it's my understanding that you all wanted me transported to Alaska, where I would become a part of the HAARP program's research. Is that correct?" Phoenix wiped his mouth with the corner of his sleeve after his search for a napkin proved useless.

Deutch took a breath and cleared his throat. "Sergeant Major, we transported you to a remote area in Alaska where we believed you would be hidden from anyone wanting to cause you harm."

Phoenix chuckled, then slammed his fist on the table. "Star Gate wasn't your only gig. You sent me there to kill me. You sent me there to study me like a fucking lab rat at HAARP until you could arrange my death in Bosnia, didn't you, Director?"

The director stepped back. "No! You were there. You saw it. You were sent to Srebrenica because nobody else could get those hostages out of there!"

"Who planted the IED's, Mr. Deutch? Who fucking planted the IEDs?"

"What the hell are you talking about?" The director shook his head, looking stunned, his eyes fiery and his brows furrowed.

"I'm talking about the research. I know what you've been doing all along. All of you. I don't know how many of you are behind this, but I will not be a part of your damn cloning program." Phoenix lifted another chunk of meat to his mouth. He relished the taste of prime rib and maintained calm while the director wrestled with visible unease.

Phoenix still had the upper hand, only because the feds had not yet developed a way to penetrate a human mind. It was the only source of privacy that he still had. The privacy of his thoughts. But if Russia and the USA could develop a way to clone their respective superhumans, mind control and invasion would become a future reality.

"Sergeant Major, the research behind human cloning didn't start with you. It's been going on for years. If you think that---

"Your research at Stanford Institute is flawed, Mr. Deutch." Phoenix interrupted.

The director darted his eyes toward the doctor, who now glared at Phoenix through squinted eyes. The doctor was stoic as he waited for Phoenix to continue. O'Connor realized that there was nothing that Phoenix could not penetrate if he willed it. Because Phoenix was able to teleport at will, he could be anywhere at any time. There was no way to control him. HAARP had been a last resort and would have worked if the hostage situation in Bosnia had not foiled the plans.

The director finally responded to Phoenix, playing the dumb card. "Which research are you referring to, Sergeant Major?"

Phoenix leaned back in the chair and pushed his plate away from the edge of the table. He pulled a napkin out from under a butter knife resting on the food tray and wiped the corners of his mouth. He then cocked his head to the side and looked at the director. He lifted his index finger in the air and pointed at Deutch as he spoke.

"You people have been studying my type of abilities for years, trying to duplicate the phenomena or manipulate it through lab experiments. Your present research, which involves measuring a soldier's thoughts before he speaks, will cause unnecessary casualties. You are attempting to take a human being and turn them into some sort of robotic war machine that reacts on cue. Humans are not wired that way. We are too complex." Phoenix waited for the doctor's response.

"Our technology is better served in robotics, not a biological living organism." The doctor interjected.

Phoenix nodded.

"The research at the Stanford Institute goes beyond remote viewing, Sergeant Major. If you are referring to the Army's special programs, I must tell you that the latest program has shown great progress, but the technology is not something that we can share. Not even with other scientists that we have contracted to assist in classified projects."

"It won't work," Phoenix stated without resolve.

"And do you think that you have the ability to train our remote viewers? Do you think that you can do a better job than the teams we have in place? You know how to read minds, Sergeant Major. You know how to make things move. But can you teach the skill to others? To those agents whom we have hand-selected and tested to be highly capable of producing the supernatural phenomena? We've put decades of time into our people and these programs. Casting the current research aside as a folly is a pretty arrogant position to take, Sergeant Major."

The sergeant major watched the director and then continued. "Mr. Deutch, arrogance has nothing to do with my position. I make my argument as a man who has lived his lifetime with these supernatural abilities. Abilities that I have strengthened and developed on my own. What you are trying to do is duplicate a natural occurrence that's guaranteed to produce a synthetic outcome. As far as teaching others, I haven't even given that a thought. You people dropped me off in Alaska expecting me to be forgotten, but then I bypassed the door and those sealed files in the bunker's main office. I scanned at least fifty documents pertaining to HAARP and the research being conducted at Stanford. And this idea of moving my ass to Homey Airport, where you expect me to make my new home with a family of fucking genderless green midgets, is utter bullshit."

The doctor looked down at the floor to keep from laughing out loud. The sergeant major's unintended comic relief was well needed in a roomful of angst. O'Connor decided it was a good time to get Phoenix out of there and underground.

"Sergeant Major, we need to get you out of here now. Part of the reason that you were transported to Alaska was to avoid the media. You're too close to the capital. General Monroe fucked us in a nuclear kind of way when he sold this country out to Russia. We need a really good story that we can sell to the media and the world. A story without you in it. Do you understand?" The doctor leaned forward and stared at Phoenix with one eyebrow cocked.

Phoenix flinched, then turned stone cold as he stared back at O'Connor. He read the doctor's thoughts. *They wanted him dead.*

Phoenix cleared his throat before speaking. "Let's get the hell out of here then." The sergeant major stood and turned toward the door.

The doctor pushed his chair back and walked around the table to join Phoenix. Deutch stopped the doctor as Phoenix reached for the door handle. "Take the tunnel out of here. He doesn't need to be seen exiting the building."

The doctor nodded and replied. "Of course."

O'Connor knew what was coming in the next few hours. He wondered if Phoenix had read the thoughts of everyone in the room, or had they been successful at confusing him? Although the doctor was on Phoenix's side and the only person whom he could trust, he had to play the game until Phoenix was capable of taking control. Dr. O'Connor knew that the feds would never be able to control Phoenix. But how far were they willing to go to get what they wanted?

"And get him a damn shower, will you? He smells like piss." Deutch ordered in a disdainful tone.

The doctor ignored the director's arrogant remarks and shut the door behind him. Phoenix looked at Dr. O'Connor as they entered the hallway leading out. The armed guard immediately led them into an elevator. He inserted a key into the elevator's interior panel, then entered a secret code into a numeric pad. The elevator doors shut and began the descent eight stories beneath the earth's surface. For the next 24 hours, Sergeant Major Seth Phoenix would be completely shut off from the outside world and the sole property of the United States of America.

CHAPTER 10

Foreign Intelligence Service Headquarters
Yasenevo, Russia

Special Agent Nikita Oleshun felt the brunt force of an officer's fist against the back of her neck as she fell to the floor. She quickly pushed her hands out in front of her to catch herself before slamming against the hard, polished tiles. Her eyes began to gloss over as her hands now stung from the impact, and she quickly tuned into the silent communication within the minds of those surrounding her.

A trickle of blood dripped down her neck where the officer's fingernail had lanced the delicate skin behind her right earlobe. She was about to be ambushed by the SVR if she didn't act fast. The prime minister and former KGB stood over her, glaring at her through wide eyes that transferred a fatal warning to Russia's most coveted spy. Although the Russian government knew the magnitude of her supernatural capabilities, she had been at the forefront of their research and under their control for more than a decade. And they weren't about to sacrifice a breach of trust even from the likes of her.

Her eyes quickly scanned the area around her, and she saw that she was surrounded by dozens of armed agents whose weapons were now deadlocked on her. She breathed deep and slow, trying to calm herself and lower her blood pressure as she looked down at the barrels of the rifles. If she made any sudden moves, she knew that they would pummel her with bullets and leave her body covered in more holes than a block of Swiss cheese. Her powers were strong, but she wasn't stupid, and she knew better than to test the men before her.

Nikita slowly moved her legs up toward her chest and began to push herself upright. As she began to stand, she looked up and locked stares with the piercing blue eyes of the prime minister. He watched her, unrelenting in his desire for domination. Nikita acknowledged his commanding presence and blinked once. She offered no other sign of submission, instead beginning to mentally record the scene as a computer processes an encrypted message. As her mind raced to sort through the incoming data, a plan of escape began to formulate. She felt her adrenal glands spike, releasing the coveted hormone that keeps her alive during recovery. Her body jerked in response, and at that moment, she parted her lips to speak.

"Prime Minister," Nikita said to Putin in a tone that invited dialogue between them. She refused to remove her eyes from his but continued her stance with a softened look as she waited for his response.

Putin breathed in and stepped back, turning his head to the side as he sized her up, a move that defined his displeasure and foreshadowed the tone to come. "Did you think that you could fool us, Nikita? Did you think that we would not know?"

Nikita remained still, not daring to move an inch. Her body became ravaged with fear as she stood painfully stiff before him. *What if Putin didn't believe her?*

"There was an explosion, Mr. Putin. I saw the American. Sergeant Major Seth Phoenix. I saw him enter the building, and I saw the hostages being removed, but--"

Nikita waited. Putin turned and looked back at the president and the agents surrounding him with pointed weapons. He then leaned forward toward her. "And your mission was to gather intelligence about this Phoenix. Your mission was to collect a sample of his DNA." His tone was barely above a whisper as he spat the words in Russian and clenched his teeth.

Then, without warning, he yelled, slamming his fist in the air. "And you brought us nothing! You brought us nothing!" The prime minister repeated, causing Nikita to flinch. She felt a drop of spittle land against her cheek.

"The explosion—it—there was nothing left. The American was still inside." Nikita hesitated, stumbling over her words, but her tone sounded convincing. *How could they know if she had communicated with Phoenix?* She had been tracking Phoenix alone.

Prime Minister Vladimir Putin became quiet. He studied her. Just minutes before, the Russian agent had exited the Mil M24 that had transported her to the Russian intelligence and espionage headquarters situated in the center of a Russian forest in Yasenevo. He had watched her from the windows of the second-floor office as she exited the aircraft. He watched her body language as she made her way to the doors leading into the Y-shaped campus that housed some of the most sophisticated intelligence systems in the world.

The country's most skilled intelligence officers had tracked Oleshun during the explosion, and Putin had been briefed on her movements outside of Srebrenica. The Russians trusted no one. Not even their own mother. Regardless of what Nikita Oleshun meant to the Russian government, she was treated as a potential threat capable of exposing Russia's most guarded secrets.

Putin stood before her with his hands clasped in front of him. "We know you were there." He stated matter-of-factly. "We also know that you hid out in a cave about a half mile in the hills overlooking Srebrenica."

Nikita said nothing but continued to stare into the prime minister's eyes. She guarded her reactions with extreme caution, careful not to reveal any telling body language in response to Putin's claims. The prime minister's remarks now confirmed her worst fear. She realized that the Russians had planted a tracking device on her body during one of her remote viewing sessions. She felt the flow of wet blood that had oozed onto her throat, but she hesitated to check the source. She suspected that the device was located somewhere on her head, and she knew that she had to locate it and remove it, but not without a plan of escape first. The SVR would be watching every move she made, even the number of times she chewed her food and emptied her bladder.

Nikita spoke in a hoarse voice. Her throat produced a scratchy, exhausted tone. "Yes, I used the cave for surveillance before I went in, and then I escaped to the same location after the explosion. Phoenix was inside when the

Serbs stormed from the back of the building. There must have been a dozen homemade bomb devices." Nikita shook her head while remembering the magnitude of the explosion, then continued. "I got out of there just as I watched the last of the American agents running for cover. There is no way he could have survived such a massive explosion. It leveled parts of that building." Nikita's tone was straightforward and showed no signs of deception, but the president wasn't convinced. He cut his eyes toward Putin and put his hand over his lips, resting his chin in his palm as he paused for a moment and contemplated what the special agent had just told them. She had been convincing, but President Yeltsin wanted Nikita to understand the consequences of betrayal. He straightened his stature and then turned to walk away from the scene. He took two steps, then halted and addressed the prime minister.

"Mr. Putin, please inform Ms. Oleshun of Russia's expectations for her. And make sure she understands."

A cold chill swept over Nikita. At that moment, she vowed to escape the country or die trying, but staying there was no longer an option.

"Yes, Mr. President, of course."

Putin waited for the door to close behind Yeltsin, then turned back toward Nikita. He stepped close toward her and faced her. He motioned for one of the agents to join his side. A tall, dark Russian man stepped forward and lowered his weapon. Putin gave the man his order and spoke under his breath, hoping that Nikita would not hear him. The dark-haired Russian then stepped forward. Although he was not touching her, he leaned toward her right side and bent close to her ear, his lips almost touching her earlobe. He spoke in a cold and malevolent tone.

"If you're lying, we're going to take that superhuman brain of yours and feed it to the pigs. Do you understand?"

Nikita's heart raced, and her scalp began to tingle as her telekinetic energy spiked. She wanted to kill him right there, but she would have to fight all of them. They outnumbered her in this moment. They had the upper hand. For the time being.

Nikita's mouth fell slightly open, and she breathed deeply. She nodded and muttered the word, "Yes."

"You can get out of here now, Ms. Oleshun. We'll be in touch."

Nikita let out a quiet sigh and closed her eyes, then quickly opened them. She began to walk toward the door as the army of agents moved aside while she exited the room. Putin followed close behind her and instructed the commander in charge to deliver Ms. Oleshun to her apartment, located just two miles away.

As the SVR agent escorted her to a Russian military transport vehicle, she attempted telepathic communication with Sergeant Major Seth Phoenix, now located eight stories beneath the earth's surface.

CHAPTER 11

Nikita's body was stiff, and she didn't dare move during the two-mile ride to her home. She stared ahead as if in a catatonic state and continued to use her mental powers to push through time and space as she attempted to reach Sergeant Major Seth Phoenix. She called out to him through her telepathic channels and repeated the urgent message to ensure it was delivered. Phoenix must hear her. He must be made aware that she would be arriving in the city by his name. She would be flying ito Phoenix, Arizona. It was a nonstop flight from Russia to a destination close to where the sergeant major was reportedly being moved. She had telepathically picked up data that indicated Seth Phoenix was going to be transported to Homey Airport. If it was right, she wanted to be there. She knew the sergeant major's intentions. She had seen them through their exchange back in the hillside cave in Srebrenica. And she wanted the same freedoms, but she was now running for her life.

She heard mental static and realized she was tuning into the underground tunnel where Phoenix was now resting. Mental images zoomed in and out of her brain's visual cortex, recording Phoenix's sensory data that translated to his current moods and physiological status. Nikita took a slow, deep breath, careful to keep it unnoticed by her escorts. Her eyes narrowed as if she was blinded by a bright light as she deciphered the information that she was receiving. Phoenix was in restoration. She observed the past hour of his time in the tunnel and concluded that he had been fed and questioned by a government official overseeing his medical care. She watched a snapshot in time as the doctor started an IV in Phoenix's left arm. And then just as she was about to call out to the sergeant major, the driver made a sudden turn that broke her train of concentration. She was within yards of her home's front door. The sudden movement of the SUV caused her body to slide over, almost touching the Russian agent, who now turned and glared at her. His eyes were as cold as ice and issued a warning meant not only to intimidate the female spy, but also to dominate and declare his self-proclaimed supremacy. She quickly slid back to the right and sat up against the passenger side door. She jerked her head around and stared straight ahead as she attempted a final and urgent call to Sergeant Major Seth Phoenix.

Like a radio blasting a warning signal, Nikita's voice raced through an invisible network. While Phoenix reclined on a cot inside the bunker's medical hall, her signals traveled faster than the speed of sound until they crossed over, penetrating outside barriers and passing directly into his brain's sensory canals. Just as the last snippets of Nikita's message rocketed forward, the sound of her voice caused his eyes to fly open and his feet to lift off the chair.

In a flash, Phoenix looked all around the room. Nikita's voice had come through like a loud siren. In fact, the sound of her voice seemed to bounce off the walls, creating an echo. He wondered whether the doctor had witnessed the same phenomenon he had just experienced. But the doctor seemed oblivious to it as he continued writing in an unidentified file. Phoenix then settled back onto the chair and listened. He waited, and he listened. And then in a split second, he answered her back.

Near the Moscow Metro, Yasenevo

The driver turned into the apartment community parking lot and stopped near the entrance to Nikita's front door. The area was well obscured by the night sky, but the agents already knew exactly which apartment Nikita lived in and even how many steps it took to reach her front door from the sidewalk.

The six-foot-four, two-hundred-thirty-five-pound Russian loyalist and foreign spy slammed the gear shift into park and hastily got out of the car as the other agent opened the back door and reached into the vehicle, pulling Nikita out by the arm and onto her feet. Both men stood behind her and motioned for her to leave, but they watched her like a hawk until she entered the building. The men then turned, got back into the SUV, and drove away, but not far. She didn't doubt for a second that she was being tracked, not only by the device that she was about to remove but also through other means of surveillance. They were watching her apartment from all four directions and even the sky.

Once inside, Nikita immediately began preparing for departure. A secret and urgent escape that would likely get her killed unless she was able to remove the small device implanted beneath her skin. The Russians had managed to plant it behind her right earlobe, in the soft crevice of skin folds. It was a smart location for a tracking device since she had not detected its presence until the brunt force of the Russian officer's fist had loosened and cracked open the skin. Even during her daily bathing regimen, she had not detected the tiny, wire-looking apparatus that fit snugly in the back bend of her ear.

The top-secret agent now stood in front of the bathroom sink. She traced her index finger along the right ear, and after a few tries, she detected it beneath her skin. She winced as she bent her earlobe forward and leaned closer to the mirror so that she could examine its location. Her eyes widened as she saw the wire that had been tracking her every movement. It was there, just barely visible under a thin layer of skin and blood. As she examined the area, she realized that the device had been placed there so easily that it was no surprise it had gone unnoticed. She had not even felt it being surgically implanted.

Nikita flicked open a pocketknife and pricked the skin with the wire tip. A small trickle of blood oozed out of the opening that now exposed the end of the wire as Nikita used a pair of tweezers to grasp hold of it and pull it away from the skin. She had to be prepared to make her exit as soon as the wire was removed because the Russians would know that she had located the tracking device. Nikita laid the wire down and quickly placed a tissue against the small hole, applying pressure to stop the bleeding. She then grabbed a backpack and stuffed it with a fake ID, a change of clothes, and a box of protein snacks. She then hauled ass toward the back door. Every move she made had to be three steps ahead of the Russians stalking her. She had to use her abilities to know everything they were thinking and planning. She even had to know the precise moment when her stalkers were sneaking a few blinks or a glance down at the ground that would allow her to slip by unnoticed. And at this fateful moment, she seized the opportunity when the Russian hiding at the corner of the apartment complex looked down at the ground and rubbed his nose. At that moment, she scurried down two flights of stairs, unscathed and undetected. The next few hours would become the ultimate test of her abilities as she boarded a plane for the Land of Dreams.

CHAPTER 12

Sheremetyevo International Airport
Moscow, Russia

Nikita quickly pushed the taxicab door open and exited the back seat after paying the cab fare for the forty-minute ride. Her feet moved with phenomenal speed as she zipped past security guards. For every blink or distraction they yielded to, she was right there reading it seconds before it happened. The minor infractions allowed her to escape past them without being seen or heard. She knew the Russians were now scrambling to intercept her, and if they succeeded, she would be dead.

She blended in with the hundreds of travelers all hurrying to catch their flights. She raced to the ticket kiosk and rushed to purchase a one-way flight to Phoenix, Arizona. She pulled out a fake ID and a credit card in the same name to make the purchase. Within seconds, the transaction was processed, and a paper ticket was dispensed. Nikita wasted no time and headed straight for the security point.

She waited in line and mentally tuned in to her surroundings. She detected no approaching interference, but she suspected that it would be only hours away, if not sooner. But just as she felt a moment of relief from her angst, a flash of insight burst forth before her eyes and alerted her to footsteps running steadfast toward her. She jerked around and made a dash for the restroom, leaving her place in line empty for the man behind her. She breathed fast as she walked into a stall and stood on top of the toilet seat. She slammed the door shut and knelt, closing her eyes and reading the scene, deciphering the energy of the uniformed men coming through the airport. *Security guards. Four of them. Searching for a suspect wanted in a crime committed just twenty-four hours before.*

Nikita opened her eyes and leaned her head back, her lips pursed with nervous tension. She had to remain calm. *Somehow.* She stepped down from the toilet and opened the bathroom door. Then immediately jerked backward as someone rushed around the corner to another bathroom stall.

She waited and stood still, rubbing her fingertips against the temple of her head as she concentrated once again. But this time, she focused on the interior of her apartment, attempting to detect any movement. She was stunned as she remotely viewed her living quarters. Not one thing had been disturbed since she escaped down two flights of stairs. But she knew that it wouldn't be long. She saw the SVR agents still standing watch at the property's front and rear exits. They had not been alerted by headquarters yet, but she knew that as soon as someone realized the wire had been removed, a hunt bigger than hell itself would ensue. And it was coming. Within minutes.

The Russian Foreign Service Agent walked out of the stall and exited the restroom. She didn't bother to survey the area as she took her place back in line again and placed her backpack on the conveyor belt. She waited until the guard motioned for her to walk through, then handed over her ticket for one last pass. Then, without hesitation, he motioned for her to move forward. Nikita had managed to bypass security points. By now, the Foreign Intelligence Headquarters was most likely discovering the missing link to Nikita Oleshun and ordering her to be assassinated on sight.

Nikita hurried, her feet almost airborne across the airport's high-gloss polished floors. She skipped three steps at a time up the escalator and made the final turn toward her boarding gate. As she neared the area, she saw the gate attendant lift the microphone to his mouth and announce the final boarding call. Within two swift steps, Nikita Oleshun was passing in front of him, her ticket in hand as she stepped across the threshold and into the plane's main cabin. As she took a seat near the back of the plane, she took a deep breath and sighed, exhaling in silence. Then she whispered to herself. *Still alive. Nineteen hours to go.*

CHAPTER 13

Sergeant Major Seth Phoenix jerked awake and rolled over at the sound of splitting wood. He swung his legs off the reclining chair and looked from side to side, his eyes wild and his movements fast and furious as he surveyed his surroundings. But all was peaceful in the underground tunnel beneath the headquarters of the Department of Homeland Security. He looked down at his arm and noticed the bandage that had been placed where the IV had been inserted a few hours before he fell into a deep sleep after sending Nikita Oleshun a final telepathic message. Phoenix cautiously walked to the edge of the door and peered out. He listened to the silence in the bunker and realized that he had been left alone.

Without warning, another loud crash echoed in his mind. He stood straight and began to investigate the rooms in the bunker. He was receiving intel from another location, but it wasn't at Fort Meade. He stopped near the exit door where Dr. O'Connor had led him into the tunnel and froze as he zeroed in on the communication being transmitted. Like a fading radio signal, he heard the Russians messaging each other before the final blow that ripped a door off its hinges. He watched the scene through clairvoyant means as the Russian agents stormed Nikita Oleshun's apartment. They jerked open closet doors and ransacked cabinets filled with her belongings that she never intended to come back for.

Phoenix knew that he was watching the event in real time. It was happening now, and he heard the Russian commands as they ordered her killed on sight. Complete and total chaos ensued as the Russians now scrambled to find her. Dozens of agents scattered in multiple directions, with at least ten agents heading with perpetual lightning speed for the Sheremetyevo International Airport, but it was too late. The 747 had already lifted and was now within minutes of crossing into U.S. airspace.

Fifty-five miles from the Alaskan border

Nikita jerked in her seat as she received telepathic intel from the sergeant major who was now attempting to communicate with her from thousands of miles away. She leaned forward and viewed the scene across the aisles of the plane's interior cabin. Most of the passengers were now sleeping or occupied with movies and reading. All was quiet. She then leaned back and rested her head against the headrest. She closed her eyes as she envisioned Phoenix standing before her.

Using her clairaudient abilities, she listened to the sergeant major's raspy voice and southern dialect as he ordered her to stay put when the plane landed in Arizona.

Although his message was short, it was precise, and there was no misunderstanding of his warning. As Phoenix transmitted his final thoughts across an invisible network, Nikita Oleshun's body became rigid, and a cold chill swept over her. Russia didn't want the U.S. to know about Nikita's defection. They would take great care to preserve their secrets, and they were no longer interested in her return. Nikita mouthed her thoughts. *A Russian assassin would be waiting.*

CHAPTER 14

Hours later.
Phoenix Sky Harbor International Airport
Phoenix, Arizona

Sergeant Major Seth Phoenix waited for his supernatural match. The plane carrying the Russian special agent was due to land within minutes, and Phoenix was watching the tarmac through a ten-foot-high window at the terminal's gate. Phoenix left nothing behind when he exited the tunnel and made his way off the base at Fort Meade. And he didn't bother to tell anyone where he was going. He zipped past people, causing mild delays for them as he instigated annoying mishaps. In order to avoid being seen by the front staff at HSA, Phoenix sent a shock wave of air toward the security guard, sending the man's eyeglasses off his face and to the floor. As the guard scrambled to retrieve his necessary spectacles, Phoenix zipped past. Within seconds and with a supernatural disguise that only he could maneuver, he was gone and out of sight before anyone realized he was headed for Arizona. At least that's what Phoenix was hoping, since he was expected to stay underground for twenty-four hours under the doctor's care before being transported to Homey Airport the following morning. Top secret officials were then expected to inform the sergeant major of his role in the current military research programs. But Phoenix was already receiving fragments of information that were coming through as broken radio signals. It was still enough for him to make out what was transpiring as he stood waiting for Russia's number one kill target.

The 747 could now be seen at low altitudes as it made its way past the red Arizona mountains. Phoenix's pale blue eyes began to glow as he locked sights on the massive plane with its landing gear now open and ready to hit the pavement. His supernatural sight revealed Nikita sitting near the back of the plane. She appeared calm and collected. He sent her a telepathic signal that he had arrived and would be waiting as she exited the plane.

The Delta airliner made a smooth landing on the runway, with only minimal forward thrust, as the plane abruptly slowed and entered the gate. Phoenix began to pace the floor. He walked back and forth around the area and away from the line of people that had now congregated near the ticket counter, but he never took his eyes off the crowd. He watched them and invaded their thoughts as he practiced supernatural surveillance on each person within thirty feet of the exit door. He didn't detect any possible interference. Contrary to his expectations, the scene seemed almost surreal, leaving him momentarily confused and curious. There was no CIA there. No FBI. No cops or security interference. Although Phoenix was picking up bits of future conversations, it had been broken into fragments and was difficult to discern. The doctor and the CIA knew he could read their every move, but Phoenix was being played. The White House knew about Nikita Oleshun and that she was landing at Phoenix Sky Harbor International Airport.

The plane's door was thrust open, and travelers began to make their way down the ramp toward the terminal. Phoenix knew Nikita would be one of the last to de-board the plane, but he still scanned every person as each one passed through the door. At this point, Phoenix assessed every person he encountered as a potential enemy.

Just then, Nikita Oleshun stepped foot across the threshold and into the terminal. Her body tingled as her senses soared into high alert. She moved quickly through the crowd, cautiously, until Phoenix suddenly stepped forward and locked eyes with her. Nikita stopped dead still for a brief moment as she stared into her American ally's face. Her own expressions were revealing enough without the need to penetrate her thoughts. The two of them shared a chemistry beyond the biological engineering of their supernatural makeup. And it was obvious.

Phoenix tore his eyes away and quickly motioned for her to follow. There wasn't time for romantic interludes, even though he felt it all the way to his loins. Nikita wasted no time and fell in behind Phoenix as they made their way through the airport terminal and toward the escalators leading to the baggage and claims division. The two of them hurriedly placed their feet on the moving steps. She noticed the suspended airplane hanging from the ceiling, set against a backdrop of a built-in stone waterfall. The scene was one that she would never forget as she stood close to Phoenix.

As the escalator neared the ground level of the airport, Phoenix skipped a couple of steps and moved fast toward the outside doors. He then paused and turned to Nikita. Phoenix whispered; his words were hushed but precise.

"We have a greeter waiting to meet us."

Nikita nodded. "Russian assassin."

"We have to reach Homey Airport."

Phoenix knew that they had to remain almost invisible to the people around them, and it wasn't safe to use any of their telekinetic abilities even if they had to. Although the scene appeared to be clear, he knew he had to meet Nikita Oleshun's enemy in the open. He had to drag him out. If the assassin was armed as he suspected, Nikita would need help. The supernatural Russian agent was a walking bullseye, and a secret Russian assassin on American soil wasn't going home without a kill.

"What now?" Nikita took a deep breath and focused on the parking garage ahead of them.

Phoenix pushed the door open and immediately scanned the area with X-ray vision. He raised his hand in the air and motioned for her to follow. "In the car."

The base was a good eight-hour drive, including restroom stops, from the heart of Arizona. If they managed to stay alive and make it to the entrance of Homey Airport, they could consider themselves home free. The base was one of the most guarded installations in the entire world. But any unauthorized individual who stepped one foot across the restricted line could set off an ambush worse than the FBI's slaughter of Bonnie and Clyde, who took one hundred thirty rounds of steel-jacketed bullets. The only thing worse than being killed at Area 51 was being caught alive and sentenced to a federal prison where the bad boys would mind fuck a person until they were ready to kill them.

Phoenix knew that the White House wanted him kept alive regardless of the aggravation he had caused. He was on the run to save a Russian defector who had become an important ally and a trusted friend. As long as he stayed within the homeland, he was still considered a government spy with a negotiable future. That's what the president and the CIA wanted. A negotiation with the supernatural spy. If Nikita Oleshun did what CIA Director Deutch anticipated her to do, she would gladly accept an offer that would end her days on the run.

Dr. O'Connor and the research team at Stanford Institute would continue the military's paranormal research under a secret umbrella that the CIA would no longer make available to any Congressional committee. The project would continue as a black operation with no access outside the team's main operatives. And there would be a scarce paper trail detailing the program's progress.

The sergeant major and Russian secret spy entered the airport parking garage and found the Dodge Charger Phoenix had picked up from the car rental downstairs. They got in the car and slammed the doors shut, not wasting a second before speeding out around the corner and onto the highway leading straight to the Nevada desert.

The two agents were quiet for a moment, consumed by the reality of the present as they fixed their sights on the road ahead. Phoenix and Oleshun shared the gifts of telepathy, telekinesis, and clairvoyance, but none of these abilities enabled them to change a future occurrence. What it could do was allow them a chance to change a future outcome if they had time to intervene. The Russian assassin would be waiting, and Nikita now feared the confrontation. She knew he would be armed with an arsenal. Enough to kill a small army of men.

In an instant, Nikita felt a chilling revelation creep upon her, slamming into her mental faculties. She jerked around and looked at Phoenix, who met her glance.

"He's just ahead of us." Nikita's eyes were wide. Her hands trembled as she positioned her fingertips against both sides of her temples, massaging them in a circular motion.

Phoenix's eyes were squinting as he stared ahead. He zeroed in on the road ahead of him, and then, without warning, he yelled out, his body now tense as he swerved to miss the oncoming car.

"Oh, fuck! No, he's here now! Get down!"

The Russian assassin slammed into the front driver's side of the black Dodge Charger. The sound of crushing metal and screeching tires burned into Nikita's ears as she struggled to gain control of her body, being slung about. She grabbed the side door handle as her head slammed against the glass window. Her mouth gaped open, and tears streamed down her cheeks from the pain of the impact. A trickle of blood escaped just beneath her brow, and she quickly reached up and placed her hand against the fresh wound now pulsing with pain. She pulled her hand away and inspected her wet fingers, now covered in bright, crimson blood. Rage began to consume her as she viewed her own life force and the reality of a certain death staring her in the face. Instead of fear, she felt anger bubbling up inside of her, and at that moment, she wanted revenge. Revenge for the loss of years she gave the Russian government, the sacrifice, and the dedication that now was about to be extinguished. Time seemed to slow down, creating the sensation of slow motion, yet everything was actually happening in split-second speed.

"Send a shock wave!" Phoenix shouted.

"A what?" Nikita shouted back in confusion. She then pulled her knees up to her chest and turned to face the back of the car, looking out the rear window.

"Blast the fuck out of him!" Phoenix shouted, his tone now more urgent than ever as he swerved to the other lane of the highway. The assassin was fast gaining on him and was within inches of ramming him from behind.

Phoenix looked in the rearview mirror as the white 4x4 Chevy inched closer. "What the fuck?" The sergeant major struggled to keep his eyes on the truck as he zipped back and forth between the truck and the road. He noticed something situated in the passenger seat and tried to determine what the assassin had posted there. Just then, his mouth fell open as the assassin placed his fingers on the trigger of a rocket aimed dead at them.

"Get down!" Phoenix shouted, slamming the gas pedal to the floor as the car's engine roared and accelerated them forward. Phoenix fought to maintain control of the car, desperately trying to avoid a crash. But the back and forth across the lanes and the hundred-mile-an-hour speeds were leading him and his supernatural accomplice to their own grave if he didn't eliminate the Russian killer now.

At that very moment, Nikita released a supersonic wave toward the assailant. The invisible mega-force rocked the truck, crushing the front grille as the killer squeezed the release button. The rocket launched from its base, shattering the front windshield as the assailant's body fell backward.

Phoenix worked furiously to spin the car around in the opposite direction, and his palms felt the burn of the leather steering wheel as he jerked and slid it counterclockwise. The deadly rocket zoomed past, headed for the middle of nowhere until the sound of its detonation pierced the ears of its survivors. The car screeched to a sudden stop, with heat from the tires sending a cloud of smoke into the air.

Phoenix acted fast as he shook off the aftershock and pushed against the driver's side door that was now crushed in. The door latch was broken in half, and Phoenix was trapped as the Russian assailant marched in speedy haste toward him, rifle in hand and ready to fire. Phoenix pushed both his palms forward. His supernatural power pulsated forward, sending the car door flying into the air. Nikita rushed to exit the passenger side and shield herself away from the assailant's view, but just as she knelt beside the right front of the car, the assailant hurled an explosive device that had been laced with a paralyzing agent designed to disable her. One breath of the toxic chemical and she would be rendered helpless, if not dead.

Phoenix was too late. The metal canister clinked as it landed on the asphalt near the car. A putrid smell of burning rubber escaped as the vapors filled the air, indicating that the gas wasn't in its purest form. The killer was using chemical weapons of mass destruction known as Sarin, a deadly nerve agent that would destroy Nikita Oleshun's central nervous system within seconds. She would have no defense against this type of weapon, and the Russian assassin would have the dead body that he came for.

Phoenix jumped in the air and sailed over the hood of the car. His feet barely hit the ground as he grabbed Nikita by the arm. In one swift move, he threw her over his shoulder and raced away with expeditious speed. Even though Phoenix had moved with fury, both of the supernatural agents had been mildly exposed as they inhaled the vapors while fleeing the area. And Phoenix knew the chemicals' effects were now just seconds away.

He slowed to a stop and eased Nikita off his back. The mind-reading spy coughed and looked at Phoenix with a cocky smile. "Many thanks, sergeant major. Looks like we're even now."

Phoenix chose to ignore the remark and shook his head. He pointed ahead at the abandoned vehicles. The empty tin canisters that carried the deadly nerve gas lay in the middle of the road, and the Russian killer appeared to have vanished. Phoenix knew better, but he didn't want to admit to Nikita that they might not make it to Homey Airport. The Sarin that they had been exposed to was twenty-six times more deadly than cyanide, and Phoenix's pupils had already begun to constrict. He then took Nikita by the hand and lifted her chin with his other hand, holding her face at eye level with his own. He looked into the pale blue eyes that matched his own.

Nikita had to catch herself as her legs grew weak. She wanted to embrace the sergeant major at that moment. The moment when the veil had been lifted, she was allowed to walk through a door that had been closed to all others until now. For a brief moment, he let her see and feel the tenderness of his heart before he resumed a sergeant major's posture. As Phoenix pulled away and released her hand from his, he issued a final and deadly command.

"Let's kill this bastard."

Nikita stood beside him, ready to join forces. The two of them faced north and scanned the area searching for the assassin who now stalked them from a few yards away. He had managed to escape the airborne vapors and was now hiding out in the bed of the truck. The assassin picked up a Browning .50 caliber machine gun and pointed the barrel with a dead-on aim at Nikita Oleshun. The assassin tightened his fingers around the trigger and squeezed.

Phoenix tasted the salty liquid that dripped from his nose and eyelids. He then moved closer to Nikita, and in one swift motion, the two of them joined forces, their arms stretched outward, palms facing outward as Phoenix screamed, "Now!"

Although their bodies were weakening from exposure to Sarin, the two equals emitted electromagnetic pulses that produced wind speeds of up to 100 miles per hour. Nikita's eyes resonated with psychedelic blue while Phoenix's eyes glowed pale blue, almost white. Nikita's head hurt, and sweat soaked her shirt as she pummeled her energies forward. Until she heard the bullets. In her extraordinary awareness and heightened hearing ability, she heard the bullets before they were even expelled from the barrel of the .50 caliber gun.

Nikita fell to the ground. Seth Phoenix felt Nikita's energy dissipate, and he swiftly joined her as the two dodged bullets that penetrated the weakened electromagnetic wall they had built together.

From a distance, the Russian assassin felt the force of their explosion, but the winds were dying fast without a continual onslaught from the two superheroes. The roar of the magnetic blast sent the assassin off his feet and into the air. He was hurled almost thirty feet away from the truck, where he landed with a bone-breaking thud against the concrete ground. He scrambled to get up and reclaim any still-functional weapons in the back of the truck. But just as he placed a hand on the truck's tailgate and pulled himself up, he felt a powerful wind circling above him, and he heard the familiar thunderous sounds of helicopter blades.

Phoenix felt the ground vibrating beneath him. The helicopter blades chopping through the air caused him to automatically cover his head and ears. He slowly lifted his eyes upward and saw the symbol on the side of the chopper. It was a Lakota, a rescue chopper used for Med-Vac. United States Army. And following its lead was an Apache air cavalry. Where there was one, there would be more. He rolled over and touched Nikita. She was still alert but showed dangerous symptomatic signs of Sarin poisoning. Her eyes were watery, and her mouth drooled. Phoenix slowly got up on his knees and waved his hand in the air at the chopper now descending nearby.

The assassin lay frozen in the bed of the truck as he watched Phoenix rise to his knees. It was now or never. He had to kill them both. He had to fulfill the mission. He knew he would die at the hands of the Americans, but not without suffering the death of their own Sergeant Major Seth Phoenix and the Russian agent turned trader.

He scrambled out of the truck and ran fast and hard toward Phoenix. He tucked the Russian PP-19 Bizon on his shoulder as he readied himself to fire the 9mm rounds. And then with a fierce and sadistic roar, he charged forward, emptying the gun clip.

Phoenix fell over, his body now resting against Nikita as the Russian assassin stormed toward him. Hovering above them inside the chopper were two snipers positioned at the side door, rifles in hand. The snipers expedited the kill with a fury as they released an onslaught of rounds from the barrel of an AWC-G2 rifle. The Russian assailant's arms flew out as his body appeared to convulse before he fell dead.

Within seconds, the chopper was on the ground, and a rescue team of four soldiers dressed in typical camouflage gear exited the aircraft. One by one, they jumped to the ground and rushed to Phoenix's side. The two-person teams quickly lifted the sergeant major and Nikita Oleshun onto a gurney. The men then hurried to the chopper and placed the two agents in the rear, where emergency medical response was now administered.

With the two most coveted humans in the world now back in the U.S. military's hands, the chopper blades sped up, and the bird headed straight for Homey Airport. Within seconds before the chopper could clear the area, a government "cleaner" was on-site to remove the Russian assassin's dead body. The "cleaner" dressed to look like a banker in a navy-blue jacket and khaki pants slid the van door open and lifted the body into the rear of the vehicle. He then slammed the door shut, jumped back into the driver's seat, and sped away. He had a job to finish in another location, but when it was done, the Russian assassin's body would be disintegrated along with any history of his existence in the USA. It would be as if he had vanished into oblivion. Without even a trace.

CHAPTER 15

Inside Homey Airport, aka AREA 51
0607 hours

Nikita Oleshun opened her eyes and moved them from side to side as she surveyed her surroundings. She was now inside the compound of Area 51, the most guarded and highly classified military base in the entire world. Unauthorized people were not allowed within miles of the installation, and no trespassers had ever lived to talk about their discoveries.

The military had somewhat successfully denied its existence for more than four decades, but there was no denying the base's developmental programs that included the research and design of new weapon systems, otherwise known as black projects. This was the Stanford Institute's real secret. The living and breathing products of Dr. Nathaniel O'Connor's team and their experimentation. Star Gate had only been a speck on a grid map of secret ops that not only the United States Army but also all other branches of the military commanded. It was a combined effort in military science and a race to see who finished first in the highly classified paranormal studies of the human mind.

Nikita looked down toward her feet. She was covered by an army-green bedsheet. She turned her head from side to side, testing her ability to move, then drummed her fingers against the mattress. *Everything seems to be intact.* She then lifted her hands and rested them on her abdomen. She ran her hands across her pelvic area and immediately realized that she was naked underneath the sheet. She jerked her head off the bed and frantically looked around the room. As her eyes darted around the area, she noticed Phoenix on the other side of a wall with only a window separating them. He appeared to be awake, but resting.

Nikita then reached back toward her head and felt her hair. She could tell that it had been wet. She smelled the skin on her arms and detected a faint odor like some sort of detergent. The naked mystery was solved now as she realized that they had washed their bodies down after the Sarin exposure.

The sergeant major sensed someone staring at him from across the room. He turned his head to the left and met her eyes. He then casually lifted his left hand in the air and waved "hello" as if he didn't have a care in the world.

Nikita's face broke into a smile as she let out a laugh under her breath. She then touched the temple of her head with her first two fingers, signaling to Phoenix that she was attempting telepathic communication. Nikita wasn't certain if it was clear for her and Phoenix to talk aloud, and she wanted to know if they were now at Homey Airport.

Phoenix studied Nikita and listened to her thoughts as the two of them stared into each other's eyes. He heard her and responded with one slow blink. Then he answered her, and she received his response in short snippets.

Affirmative. Homey.

The Russian spy then offered a cute eye roll as she sent another telepathic message. This time, she wanted to know where the hell her clothes were.

The sergeant major looked stunned and patted the bedsheet covering him. He stared back with that "oh shit" kind of look as he glanced around searching for his own. He then raised his eyebrows and shrugged his shoulders before he peeled the bedsheet back, revealing his partially nude body. He then got out of bed and stood with his back to Nikita as she stared in disbelief at the sergeant major's no-nonsense approach to modesty.

His perfectly chiseled, round ass now faced her as her cheeks flushed pink during a moment of admiration. The sergeant major then raised his arm in the air. He made a circular motion with his hand, signaling for her to get out of bed while his back was turned, giving her some privacy.

Nikita reacted in an instant as she slung her legs to one side and lifted herself off the bed. She pulled the bedsheet around her body as she now examined a panel of flashing lights and low-toned beeping equipment near the opposite side of the room. But just as she placed one foot forward, a male voice rang out from the doorway.

"Your clothes?" The unidentified man in a white coat and wire-rimmed spectacles stepped forward and handed them over.

Nikita looked down at the freshly pressed, folded pair of Army fatigues, with a matching shirt, boots, and underwear appropriate for a woman. She offered no comment, instead nodding and accepting the clothing. The man then turned toward the window, where Phoenix was now standing, fully dressed, observing Nikita's interaction with Dr. Richard Scott, one of the leading research scientists at Homey Airport, and unknown to anyone outside Area 51.

Dr. Scott acknowledged Phoenix with a head nod and then stepped around the dividing wall and into Phoenix's room. The 6'1", blond-haired man almost stood toe to toe with Phoenix's 6'3" stature. He extended his hand in a welcoming gesture and waited for Phoenix to accept his handshake. Phoenix studied the scientist with curiosity and caution but did not hesitate to reciprocate the man's gesture. As their hands met, the scientist greeted the sergeant major with instructions.

"Welcome, Sergeant Major Seth Phoenix. We've been waiting for you and your Russian accomplice to recover from that near-death event yesterday. Please join us now, down the hall in Room 33. Your friends are waiting for you." The scientist squeezed Phoenix's hand and smiled before releasing it and turning to walk out.

Phoenix was speechless, his brows furrowed as he assessed the scientist's peculiar words. He felt as if he had just stepped into the twilight zone. *Your friends are waiting for you. What the hell did that mean?*

Phoenix looked through the wide window separating him from Nikita and motioned for her to join him at the doorway. She finished tightening her boot laces, then stood up and hurriedly skipped toward the door, joining the sergeant major. While standing arm in arm, the two of them turned the corner together and entered the dimly lit hallway leading to Room 33.

Phoenix and Nikita heard the door shut as Dr. Scott closed it behind him. Phoenix's body tingled with a heightened sense of awareness while Nikita Oleshun fought the urge to escape and run. Neither of them knew exactly what was waiting on the other side, but Phoenix did not fear for his life. He sensed something else unfolding. Something that had been hidden until now.

The sergeant major stopped outside the heavy steel door and looked at Nikita. Her blue eyes searched his.

"You are safe with me." He spoke to her in an authoritative tone as if there was no need to question anything. She closed her eyes and touched his arm as he pushed the door open.

Phoenix and Nikita entered what seemed like a roomful of eyes, as a small gathering of top-secret agents and government officials watched them pass through the door. There were no empty seats at the large conference table, which could seat up to twenty-five people.

Phoenix scanned the faces of the men now facing him and stood in stunned silence as he recognized the face of his friend, Nick Majors. The same friend he had pulled from the rubble at Fort Bragg after the explosion. Neither he nor Finley had ever caught up with Majors after he was transported to the local hospital. In fact, they never heard from him again. And now Majors was in a room at Area 51. Phoenix's thoughts almost escaped his lips. *What the fuck was going on?*

Nikita didn't move an inch as Phoenix continued to scan the left side of the room. Chief of Staff of the United States Army General Gordon R. Sullivan, reportedly now retired from the military, was seated next to Phoenix's closest ally and only trusted friend, Dr. Nathaniel O'Connor. And Dr. Richard Scott, Chief Scientist of Paranormal Studies and Weapons Systems, was standing right next to him.

"Please. Have a seat." Dr. Scott motioned for Nikita and Phoenix to take the two empty chairs at the head of the table.

Phoenix pulled the chairs back and moved aside, allowing Nikita to be seated at the same time he was. He settled into the well-padded roller chair and leaned forward, placing his arms on the table before him. His jawline was tight and his eyes piercing as he made a final sweep around the right side of the table and stopped where he locked eyes with Nick Majors. He cleared his throat and spoke in a tone his friend had heard before. It was a warning tone, and it only came before Phoenix let all hell break loose.

"What the fuck is going on here? Nick?" Majors flinched.

"Seth." Majors tried to remain calm, answering Phoenix with a short acknowledgment.

Dr. Scott tapped the table and hastily spoke up, interrupting the tense exchange. "Sergeant Major, we need to brief you on some information that you are unaware of."

Phoenix rolled his eyes around to the scientist and nodded in agreement. He wasn't omniscient, so it was not uncommon for the supernatural soldier to miss important intel unless he had a reason to tap into it using his abilities.

Phoenix leaned back and began interrogating the scientist without letting him speak. "How did you know I was in the middle of the fucking desert fighting a Russian assassin?" Phoenix had already begun reading their thoughts.

Dr. Scott cleared his throat but hesitated to speak. General Sullivan interjected. "Sergeant Major Phoenix, we've been tracking you since the attack at Fort Bragg. There hasn't been one second of your day that we didn't know your exact location."

Phoenix avoided showing any emotional response, even though he wanted to stare the general down with a hard frown. As he fought the temptation, he turned his eyes up to meet the general's and maintained a respectful gaze. He kept his temperament in check as he waited for him to continue.

"The CIA and the FBI have had a ghost tracking you at random times and in random locations. And your near-death experience in Bosnia was a setup by the Russian government. Your friend here was sent there to gather intel and a DNA sample from you. But she failed. The bombing was an inside job meant to put her close enough to you to get what they needed."

Phoenix stared back. "Sir, I already know this."

"Yes, but over the last few weeks, you discovered HAARP and other highly classified information that we cannot risk exposure of."

Phoenix shook his head in confusion. He zoomed in on his friend, Nick Majors, and invaded his thoughts. He then demanded a straightforward answer from his once-closest friend and new remote-viewing recruit.

"How long have you been a part of this program?"

Majors tensed up. "Since I got out of the hospital. They came and questioned me about your abilities and asked how long I had known you. All kinds of questions that I wasn't sure how to answer."

"And you were offered an opportunity just like that to be in the Star Gate program?"

"No. They tested me just like they did Finley. But I tested strongly in remote viewing. I could see things, Seth. And I was damn good at it." Majors emphasized his words with an awestruck tone.

"So, it's been you following me all along?" Phoenix asked his friend, who now looked down at the table.

"Yes, I saw the Russian, and I knew exactly when and where that bastard was going to ambush you. It was me who sent out the alert and got the choppers in the air."

The room was dead silent as Phoenix processed his friend's confession. He offered Nick Majors an appreciative look but declined a verbal response.

Dr. Richard Scott then spoke, breaking the silence. "We have a proposition for you, Phoenix."

Phoenix shifted into his chair. He felt a sense of dread, and Nikita responded in a like fashion as she noticed a change in the scientist's tone.

"We saved Ms. Oleshun from becoming dog food. Without our help, she will not survive. The Russians will hunt her down, but we have approval from the White House to offer her full asylum and a new identity in the United States." Dr. Scott glanced over at Nikita, then back at Phoenix.

Phoenix's eyes narrowed as he studied Dr. Scott. "What do you want?" His tone was forceful, but then in one swift motion, Phoenix put his hand out in front of him, palm facing outward.

"No, wait. I'm done. I want out. I've done my time." He shook his head as he spoke.

Dr. Scott turned and looked at Dr. O'Connor, who sat with his chin resting in his hand. O'Connor declined to speak. Dr. Scott turned back to Phoenix. He spoke with a firm and unrelenting tone as he ordered the sergeant major to kill on command.

"We want you to kill. As you are ordered to do so. You are a soldier, Phoenix. A soldier for the United States of America."

Phoenix leaned back in his chair. A sickening pain stabbed Nikita in the stomach, causing her to gasp.

Phoenix stared in disbelief. He had seen enough death and now only wanted to use his extraordinary capabilities for good. He didn't want to be anybody's assassin. He wanted to go home.

"No," Phoenix spoke with calmness, yet his tone left little to discern. He was stern. His decision was non-negotiable.

The scientist looked at him with a sideways smile and responded. "Sergeant Major, we trained you. We made you who you are. If you don't do what we ask, we can make sure you don't live to see daylight."

Phoenix jumped up and slammed his fists against the table as he leaned forward, almost touching the scientist's nose with his own.

"Don't you ever threaten me, you son of a bitch! If I can stop another man's heart from beating, what the fuck makes you think that I can't stop yours?"

Dr. Scott felt Phoenix's breath against his face and backed off.

Dr. O'Connor stood up and motioned for the sergeant major to relax. He spoke to Phoenix in a fatherly tone.

"Seth, your friend will die if she leaves this area anytime soon. With both of you heading up the remote viewing programs here, we can stop terrorism before it strikes the homeland."

Phoenix slowed his breathing and moved away from Dr. Scott. He refused to sit back down but remained standing at the head of the table. He looked down at Nikita, who sat quietly, not daring to show emotion or incite any reactions aimed in her direction. She was scared. Beyond the walls that separated them from the outside, she could see the end for her and Phoenix as dozens of armed guards waited to rip them to shreds if they resisted. In this moment, she feared everything and everybody. Except for Seth Phoenix.

"The Russian government thinks she's dead?" Phoenix posed a necessary reality for her survival as a question.

"We'll make sure that's the story the Russians hear from the ambassador."

Phoenix nodded once before informing the men inside Room 33 of his final offer. He wasn't backing off, and he didn't give a damn if he had to squeeze the life out of everybody in the room.

"Gentlemen, when I walk out that door, I want to be a free man. I refuse to be a test tube for the mad scientists of the U.S. military, and I'm damn sure not going to let you clone me into some degenerate killing machine. Do you understand?" Phoenix paused. He scanned the faces of every person at the table. Then he continued.

"Give me a place here, and I will work for the country that I have served with honor and integrity. I'm willing to do contract work for the military. I'll be your secret agent, and I'll work with Dr. O'Connor here as I always have. He's been with me since this circus started months ago. I'll help defend the homeland with Nikita Oleshun by my side, but only under those conditions. Otherwise, I'm walking out of here, and I fucking dare you to try and stop me." Phoenix glared at the scientist.

Dr. Scott turned to Dr. O'Connor, who was now fighting to hide a sense of victory on his face.

Dr. O'Connor responded to Phoenix with a nod and then spoke. "Sergeant Major, I believe that's fair. As you know, I've headed some of these programs for the past decade, and my research can't move forward without you and Ms. Oleshun on the team."

Phoenix nodded in agreement with the doctor's offer. He then reached down and took Nikita Oleshun's hand, lifting her out of the chair and onto her feet. He turned to Dr. Scott as he reached for the door.

"You can call off your watchdogs now because I'm getting the hell out of here for a few days."

Dr. O'Connor spoke in a panicked voice. "Where are you going?"

Phoenix stopped at the door and glanced back over his shoulder. "To see Abigail and Stephen Phoenix."

Dr. Scott looked at Dr. O'Connor with an inquisitive stare.

Dr. O'Connor answered the scientist's inquisitive look. "Chattanooga."

The door slowly shut behind them as Nikita Oleshun followed Phoenix out the door. She looked bewildered as she repeated Dr. O'Connor's words in a broken pronunciation. "Chatta--noo--ga?"

Phoenix laughed. "Yeah, Chattanooga."

Nikita smiled and asked. "Where is this place?"

Phoenix turned and admired her features, absorbing her beauty for a moment. Then he reached for her hand and locked his fingers in hers as they walked toward a red exit sign at the end of the hall.

"Home." The sergeant major affirmed.

Who is the fictional SETH PHOENIX?

Name: Seth Phoenix
Call name: Seth
Age: 39
Birthdate: March 21, 1956 (Born on the cusp of Pisces and Aries)
Place of birth: Chattanooga, Tennessee
Height: 6'3"
Weight: 210 lbs.
Eye color: Intense blue
Hair color: Dark Brown
Distinguishing marks: A star-shaped birthmark near his temple and hidden inside his hairline.
Special notes about Seth: He was born a star child. Possesses the ability of clairvoyance, telepathy, and telekinesis. Anger causes his energy to dissipate and become chaotic, leading to the destruction of nearby objects and the displacement of material things.
Father's name: Stephen Phoenix
Father's current status: Living
Mother's name: Abigail Phoenix
Current status: Living
Ethnic background: White/Cherokee Indian. German/Irish
Religion: Protestant
Degree of religious practice: Very spiritual but doesn't attend church regularly.
Marital status: Never married
Children: None
Police Record: None
Medical Record: Excellent. No pre-existing conditions.

Who is the factual NIKITA OLESHUN?

Name: Ninel Sergeyevna Kulagina
Call name: Nina
Age: 63 at death
Birthdate: July 30, 1926
Died: April 11, 1990
Cause: Heart Attack
Place of birth: St. Petersburg (Leningrad), Russia
Height: 5'1"   **Weight:** 110 lbs.
Eye color: Brown   **Hair color:** Dark Brown
Special notes about Nina: The former Russian Sergeant claimed she first recognized her abilities in her youth and believed she inherited them from her mother. According to Kulagina, she noticed her telekinetic abilities when items spontaneously moved around her when she was angry. She also reported that in order to manifest the effect, she required a period of meditation and a clear mind void of any interference. Upon reaching the required focus for the phenomena, she is said to have experienced sharp pain in her spine and blurred eyesight. Reportedly, storms were known to interfere with her ability to perform psychokinetic acts.
Religion: Unknown
Marital status: Married to Viktor Vasilievich Kulagina, a Russian naval engineer
Children: Three
Medical Record: Suffered a battle wound to the abdomen at age 17. (January 1944) She underwent five operations but endured chronic pain for the rest of her life.

SUGGESTED READING

Dames, Major Ed. and Newman, Joel Harry (2011).
Tell Me What You See. Hoboken, New Jersey:
John Wiley & Sons, Inc.

McMoneagle, Joseph (2000). *Remote Viewing
Secrets: A Handbook*. Charlottesville,
Virginia:
Hampton Roads Publishing Company, Inc.

Losey, Meg Blackburn, MSC.D, PH.D. (2007).
The Children of Now. Franklin Lakes, NJ:
New Page Books.

Morehouse, David (1996). *Psychic Warrior*.
New York, NY: St. Martin's Press.

Buchanan, Lyn (2003). *The Seventh Sense: The
Secrets of Remote Viewing as Told By a
Psychic Spy for the U.S. Military*. New York,
NY: Pocket Books, a division of Simon &
Schuster, Inc.

Ritchey, David (2003). *The H.I.S.S. of the A.S.P.:
Understanding the Anomalously Sensitive
Person*. Terra Alta, West Virginia: Headline
Books, Inc.

HAVE YOU HEARD ABOUT THIS STORY?

A PREVIEW of *See No Evil*

Chapter 1

Missionary Ridge. Chattanooga, Tennessee
November 25, 1863
3:00 p.m.

The sound of footsteps sliding across the grassy slope alerted the Rebel forces of an impending attack as the Federals charged up the side of the mountain, their boots heavy and marred with mud formed from the recent rain. As they pushed forward into Confederate territory, they began to shout, their roars echoing across the side of the ridge.

"Chickamauga! Chickamauga!" The Federals chanted in unison.

Confederate General Braxton Bragg stared into the face of certain victory, his deep brown eyes moistened by the chilling blast that swept over his face and caused him to step backward. It was a warning; a cold harbinger alerting him of the end as he quickly began to order his men's retreat. But the order came too late as the federal troops advanced. The Yankees had begun to charge the ridge without the order from Union General Thomas George. They had taken the advance under their own promissory and burst forth with a force so powerful that thousands of men fell to their deaths. Haunting screams could be heard as bodies tumbled hundreds of feet down the hillside, while others found their graves where they fell.

Blood splattered in every direction as bullets split skulls and severed carotid arteries. The bloody death found its mark upon the hands of some of the men still standing who, in a desperate attempt to save their best friend's life, dragged the lifeless body until their own need to survive forced them into abandonment.

Thomas Jefferson Brown, 34th Alabama Infantry Regiment, Company B, fell to his knees. He grimaced in pain as his kneecaps hit the rocky slag surface. His feet cramped inside his boots, and his arms trembled from fatigue. He held his musket tight, his head lowered, and his eyes closed as he felt the enemy's encirclement.

Just as the enemy's shouts rang loud, he felt a quick, hard thrust from the bottom of a boot. The Yankee kicked him breathless and sent his body forward as he slammed face-first into the rock. The tender skin of his left brow split open and began to bleed, the blood trickling into his eye socket.

"Get up, Soldier. Get up and fight." The Yankee mocked him and attempted to roll his body over with his foot.

Thomas Jefferson Brown was not near death, but he might as well have been. He was now a captured

Confederate soldier and a prisoner of war to the Federals. Seconds seemed like hours as his mind played back the conversation that he had with his best friend, Lewis Meadow Prater, who was serving with him. Both men had enlisted in Coosa County, Alabama. The regiment was organized on April 15, 1862, and then moved to Tupelo, Mississippi, and was placed under General Arthur M. Manigault's Brigade.

Prater and Brown had it made in Tupelo. The camp was well-guarded, and food was plentiful. They were positioned on the east side in a Confederate camp that housed several hundred men overlooking the city. It was on this hillside where Prater and Brown ate their evening supper of corn, salt pork, and bread while sitting around the glowing campfires that could be seen almost a mile away near General Bragg's headquarters. The Tupelo camps were part of what became known as the "Black Prairie" for its fertile land. Crops were easily grown in abundance, and livestock were plentiful. Thus, Tupelo and its region were capable of feeding the entire Confederate Army of the West.

On the evening before Prater and Brown were set to depart for Chattanooga, Brown unknowingly revealed a man's destiny. During the evening meal, he nudged his friend, Lewis Prater, while both men finished the last of their bread rations.

"Lewis, my good friend, I have an urgent request of you and beg for your consent." Thomas Jefferson Brown locked eyes with his closest friend as he thought of his wife back in Coosa County, Alabama. What would happen to Martha if she became a widow? How would she raise their two sons alone? Prater was his first consideration. Although

Prater was nineteen years old, he had never married and had no children.

Prater looked intently at Brown as he broke a piece of bread. "Yes, of course. What is it?"

Brown looked away and hesitated for a brief moment as he collected his thoughts, then glanced back at Prater. "I need you to promise to take care of Martha if I'm killed. I need you to promise me that you'll do it. Please. She'll be raising my sons alone. You aren't married, and it would be an honor for me."

Prater's eyes moistened as he stared into the eyes of his best friend and considered the reality that one of them might be killed within a few days. Would this be the last meal that he had with his best friend?

Prater accepted the bread that Brown passed to him. The reality of war was upon them. "I'm honored by your request. I pray that we both come home, but I will promise to take care of your family if something happens to you. You have my word." Prater stood up, and Brown joined him in front of the campfire as the two men embraced. Tears moistened the eyes of the best friends. Then Brown pulled back and looked Prater in the eyes. His hands were now clasped together as if he were about to pray. "Thank you. Thank you, my friend."

Brown's mind quickly snapped back to the present as he felt his hands bound with a leather strap. The leather stung as it was tightened around his wrists, almost cutting off the circulation. Two men hoisted him to his feet and shoved him forward, forcing him to walk down the hill where he would join over 5,000 other Confederates now destined for Rock Island, Illinois.

Chapter 2

Thomas Jefferson Brown climbed into the railcar as the other prisoners waited for boarding. Although the train was destined for the three-mile-long Mississippi River Island known as Rock Island, Illinois, it would take several days to arrive as a few hundred at a time poured into the camp. And by January 9th, 1864, just a few weeks after the Union victory at Missionary Ridge, all 6,158 captured Confederates had arrived.

The prison camp had already been notified to expect an influx of prisoners from the battle at Missionary Ridge. On November 24, just one day before the battle, a guard assigned at the prison reported that he had "no blankets, no record book, no water in the prison yard, or clothing of any kind for the Confederates". And yet the prisoners were still boarded onto the railcars and transported to what would become for many their final destination.

Brown sat cramped in the middle of dozens of other soldiers piled almost on top of each other in the railcar. Although the conditions were not comfortable, the dozens of men cramped together generated enough body heat to help alleviate some of the bitter cold that seeped through the cracks in the railcar's door. And as the train traveled farther north, crossing Indiana and much of Illinois, the train's lonely whistle faded into the sound of the howling wind as it slapped against the outside railcar's wall.

Brown's stomach churned and ached from lack of food, and he was becoming dehydrated. The cut above his left brow had finally ceased bleeding, but the stinging pain lingered as tiny pebbles of dirt and rock covered the open wound.

His mind drifted back to the battlefield. He remembered seeing the coattail of General Braxton Bragg at a distance as he narrowly escaped capture and certain death. The general's 5'10" slender frame faded into the background of his army's dead or captured men that now scattered the landscape. Brown remembered the general overseeing the camps in Tupelo, the headquarters of the Confederate Army of the West, where he had spent the last several months before the day came when Bragg sent word to General Manigault that his brigade would depart by train the following day for Chattanooga, Tennessee. He now longed to feel the warmth of his wife's touch, but his heart had known since the day he left Alabama that he might never see those comforts again, and Tupelo might become the only remaining semblance of home.

Hours turned into days as the train passed through depots heavily lined with young recruits waiting to replenish the Union army. The men's morale hit an all-time low as the reality of their demise became certain. The "Cause" was undoubtedly hopeless as they contemplated a war that never seemed to end.

The train's wheels squealed against the steel rails as it came to a halt near the prison camp. The heavy steel doors slid open, exposing daylight and mounds of glittering white powder that reflected the sun's light against a backdrop of ice-laden trees. The men's eyes were squinting as they emptied the boxcar, falling into snow two feet deep.

Brown struggled to put one foot in front of the other as he started the fourth of a mile trek toward the prison camp. Of the four hundred plus men that arrived with him, dozens of them found themselves barefoot in knee-deep snow and fighting temperatures unlike anything they had ever experienced in the South's steamy climate. It was a different kind of hell. A hell where freezing to death or suffering frostbite to the feet was a common occurrence. With no blankets or clothing for Confederate soldiers who were already thinly clad, there was little hope of survival.

Brown finally reached the barracks, which typically held 120 men, with three tiers of bunks. With the temperature registering just above freezing at 35 degrees Fahrenheit, Brown was shivering so violently that he could barely stand on two feet. He stumbled inside the building, hardly equipped to house hundreds of soldiers. The roof was all that separated the men from the night sky and the falling snow. There was no ceiling, and little protection against the elements other than the walls that blocked the icy gusts of wind swirling and howling outside.

Brown followed the line of men until he reached the bunk now designated for him. He fell against the bed and curled into a ball as dozens of his Confederate friends did the same. Within minutes, exhaustion overtook his body, and his eyes closed.

By morning, Thomas Jefferson Brown joined the ranks of those who died within the walls of Rock Island, Illinois, prison. Cause of death: exposure. His body lay motionless and hard like a block of ice. His fingers were unable to be pried open from the balled-up fists that he held onto as his hands turned blue and slowly froze solid. The gash on his eye was no longer an open cut, but rather icy and sealed shut with traces of dried blood that had trickled down the side of his left cheek. Thomas Jefferson Brown would not suffer. His end had come fast, unlike many of the others who would spend months fighting disease and freezing temperatures.

Days later, Prater received word of his best friend's death, making him the benefactor of Thomas Jefferson Brown's family, just as he had promised. While Brown's death was tragic, it was this destiny that was paving the way for a boy to be born four years later on April 21st, 1867, in Coosa County, Alabama. Because of his commitment to Thomas Jefferson Brown, Lewis Prater would father a child destined to leave behind a legacy and a gift that only God could understand and the Devil could seek to destroy.

Chapter 3

The Gordon Hotel
January 1880
Aberdeen, Mississippi

Seymour Prater stood outside the majestic red brick hotel located on East Commerce Street in Aberdeen, Mississippi. It had been years since Lewis Prater had married his best friend's widow and fathered a child with her. The couple lived in Alabama for a few years after the War of the States ended and during Reconstruction. They then moved to Monroe County, Mississippi, where the roots of Seymour Prater's supernatural legacy would be planted.

The small southern town of Aberdeen was located on the banks of the Tombigbee River, where explorer Hernando De Soto had once camped. It survived the Civil War with most of its buildings still intact, and the town now boasts a population of over 2,300 people.

Seymour gazed up at the second floor of the hotel, admiring its grandeur. It was the finest hotel along the Tombigbee Riverbanks in North Mississippi. And it served the area well since Aberdeen was one of Mississippi's busiest ports in the land where cotton was king.

He put one foot onto the front walkway leading into the hotel and stopped. He quickly leaned back just in time to avoid being hit in the face as the door swung open. Patrons of the hotel, one right after another, followed past the open door to the horses and buggies that lined the front outside entrance. Seymour watched as three, then five, men dressed in charcoal gray, pinstripe suits and matching top hats exited the hotel. As the last man stepped forward through the doorway, Seymour rushed inside, letting the door swing back against him.

John Davenport, Captain of the Tombigbee River boat *Johnson*, stepped inside The Gordon Hotel for the first time since its opening day. The interior first floor was bustling with shoppers and patrons visiting the hotel for a haircut in the barbershop or to browse the various merchant shops, where they might purchase a fine, tailored gentleman's suit or a handcrafted leather hat and matching shoes, now affordable thanks to their recent cotton trade. But Davenport's mood was heavily laden with doubt and anxiety as he mulled over an uncertain future since preparing for his final voyage down the Tombigbee River. He had been enlisted to oversee the Hargrove's estate for the past few years, transporting cotton when the river water levels allowed. Today, the riverboat was forced to dock overnight as the river's water level registered just below the ten-foot depths that were considered safe for travel to Columbus, Mississippi. With overcast skies and heavy rain expected by nightfall, the trip would most likely become navigable by mid-morning.

Davenport lifted his hat and raked strands of hair away from his eyes. He pushed the hat back down, fitting it against his head, and stood still with one hand on his hip as he glanced around the giant open area of the first floor. His eyes circled the room as he admired the decorative grandeur. The hotel's front desk was lined with guests checking into the area's newest and finest lodging place along the upper Tombigbee River. Hundreds of passengers from the many Tombigbee Riverboats had already visited the hotel within weeks of its "Open for Business" announcement. The hotel had been made possible by investors, who promised its tenants a prosperous future. Among the many occupants were entrepreneurs such as grocers, clothing merchants, barbershops, and the local newspaper, The Aberdeen Weekly.

Davenport walked to a nearby sitting area decorated with fancy, carved wooden chairs upholstered in plush red velvet cushions. He sat down and examined his boots that were covered with dust from the nearby street. He was in the wrong place. The hotel and the likes of it were much too fancy for him and his blood. He was a riverboat captain who spent many years sleeping in a bunk barely equipped to house his tall, large frame. He was used to uncomfortable conditions, and it was a life that he had become accustomed to. The scenic route along the flowing riverbanks was a pristine setting where raccoons played, deer roamed, and the occasional glimpse of a panther climbing a low-hanging tree branch sent a rapid heartbeat as it locked eyes with Davenport.

His heart was on the Tombigbee River, and the thought of this being his last trip for Mr. W. H. Hargrove caused him much grief since the railroad would now be the main means of transportation for Hargrove's cotton. Would his riverboat find more work, possibly transporting other goods to the area or even as far south as Mobile?

The young Seymour Prater watched people come and go from a corner of the hotel lobby where he positioned himself away from the traffic and inquisitive eyes of the hotel staff. He was a quiet kid with a curious nature who rarely missed an opportunity to help someone or offer advice that seemed well beyond his youthful years. He had never understood his bizarre ability to "see" into the nature of others and even determine their destinies through mental pictures that played out in his mind. And he had never told anybody about his uncanny gift for fear of ridicule or disbelief. It was an oddity that he endured alone, except when he "felt" the need to share an insight that could not be withheld within his good conscience.

Seymour watched through the storefront window as his mother shopped in one of the grocery markets inside the hotel. Martha Prater savored the smell of fresh bread as she quickly lifted it to her nose before placing it into her basket.

She joined dozens of other women this morning, eager to shop among the hotel's many venues, and she had allowed Seymour to accompany her to the hotel since she would most likely need his assistance to carry her bags.

An invisible prompt suddenly caused Seymour to look away and turn his eyes toward John Davenport, sitting in a chair across the room. He studied the man's expression and the way his body leaned forward in the chair, not sitting all the way back. He watched as the man studied his own feet. He noticed him bend over and down as he wiped his first two fingers across the toe of his boot before examining the rug beneath his feet.

Seymour's uncanny gift of insight came alive at that moment as he received the man's thoughts as invisible messages. It was as if he was plugging into a radio frequency that only John Davenport could hear, yet Seymour was an unknown invader who, regardless of his harmless intent, could no longer control his own inclinations to see into the lives of others than he could control his body's natural urges of hunger or excretion.

Davenport's anxiety was real. He thought about the possibility of the railroad now taking over as a main means of transport. He knew that his security had been threatened. And while Davenport's thoughts filled the rafters of his mind, Seymour Prater listened in as the static became clearer. What would he do with the last two decades of his life now gone? He was a river captain, and John Davenport could not conceive of any other identity.

Seymour watched Davenport and sensed a need to address him. Flashes of insight in the form of pictures now flooded his mind. He became compelled to walk across the room and sit in the chair opposite and facing Davenport. Seymour ran his hands over the plush velvet seat of the chair, feeling its soft texture and admiring how the scarlet color seemed to shift as he brushed his fingers back and forth.

Davenport glanced over at the young man sitting across from him and watched him with the same curiosity that had led Seymour across the room. What had brought the kid into the hotel lobby? Was he a runaway? Davenport studied the youth's demeanor for a few seconds before greeting him.

Davenport nodded and spoke in an even, friendly tone. "Good morning, young man. What brings you to this fine hotel?"

The corners of Seymour's mouth turned upward into a friendly smile. "Good Morning, Sir. This is my first visit to the hotel since it opened. I'm just waiting here for my mama while she shops." Seymour pointed toward one of the hotel storefronts.

"Ah, ok." Davenport nodded.

"You're a river captain, aren't you?" Seymour's inquisitive nature took over, relinquishing his otherwise shy disposition.

Davenport watched the boy's face. There was something odd about him in an uncanny kind of way. He looked to be about eleven years old, but his mannerisms, like the way he rubbed his eyes when he talked and the way he turned his head before he spoke, echoed the body language of someone much older. Like an elderly man. Yes, he reminded Davenport of an old man.

"Yes, I am. I've been a riverboat captain—

"For over twenty years. Your home is on the river." Seymour interrupted, finishing his sentence. He paused and then continued to disclose glimpses of the mental images he had witnessed a few moments earlier.

"I saw you on the riverboat *Johnson*. You work for Mr. Hargrove, but you're scared that you won't have a job in a few months when he starts using the railroad. Don't worry." Seymour paused as Davenport stared in disbelief.

"Who are you, Kid? How do you know this?" Davenport leaned back in his seat and took a deep breath.

"I'm nobody, Sir. I just have some sort of odd talent, I guess." Seymour looked away and studied his hands folded in his lap.

"What do you mean that you 'saw me on the riverboat Johnson'?" Davenport was quickly forming an opinion about the boy, but he had questions of his own.

"Oh, I just meant that I saw you in my mind. That's all." Seymour rubbed his fingers across his brow.

"You saw me in your mind? Can you see other things?" Davenport was now intrigued. He was well aware of Seymour's rare natural talent. He had only known one other person in his lifetime with the 'gift', but the former slave girl who lived on the Hargrove Plantation had been dead for years. Before being stricken with Typhoid Fever, she was considered to be Hargrove's most prized possession and often advised Master Hargrove of unseen troubles on the horizon. He had witnessed the supernatural wonders of her insights many times, and she had confided in Hargrove and Davenport, who were often by his side more than anyone else in his circle. Davenport knew how she kept her abilities sharp. He knew what she was doing each morning before sunrise when she left the cabin and walked twenty feet to the old tree stump overshadowed by hanging vines and honeysuckle blooms. He had seen her sitting there with her eyes closed, not saying a word. Just still and quiet for several minutes until it was time to return to the morning's work at the plantation mansion.

"Yes, Sir. I see pictures. Not all the time, but I started seeing pictures of you almost as soon as you entered the hotel. And I knew that I should tell you not to worry." Seymour spoke barely above a whisper as people passed near them on their way to the hotel's front check-in counter.

Davenport sighed with relief and lifted his hat as he combed his hair back once again before standing to leave the hotel. He looked at the youth now standing before him in the hotel lobby. Seymour Prater had given him an important and timely message. He had offered encouragement and hope. And now Davenport knew that he must instruct Seymour Prater about the reality of his visions. He must instruct him to develop his abilities.

"What's your name, Kid?" Davenport reached out and patted Seymour on the shoulder.

"Seymour. Seymour Prater, Sir."

"Well, my good man, Seymour, it wasn't an accident that our paths crossed today. You understand that, don't you?" Davenport looked hard and straight in Seymour's eyes.

"Yes, Sir. I believe so."

"Good. Then here's what you need to do from this day forward and for the rest of your life. You must develop this special gift that you have. It will be your calling in life. You understand?"

Seymour nodded. "Yes, but I don't know how."

Davenport motioned for Seymour to step aside as hotel guests began to take the now-empty seats that they had vacated. They took a few steps forward and stopped near the hotel's front door.

Davenport spoke clearly. "You must learn how to clear your mind and focus, Young Man. It's called meditation. You must practice this for a few minutes every day. It will open channels to you. First, find a quiet place to be alone and focus on a question in your mind, then be quiet and wait."

Seymour nodded in spite of the slight bit of confusion that he was feeling. He repeated Davenport's instructions. "Focus and clear my mind."

"Yes, that's right. I've only known one other person who could do it. And you will get better at it as time goes by. Now I have to get going. You do what I told you." Davenport patted Seymour once again on the back and reached for the door handle.

Seymour stood still in the doorway as he paused and watched John Davenport walk out ahead of him. Davenport looked back over his shoulder one last time and nodded as he spoke. "Focus. Good luck, young man." He turned the corner at the north end of the hotel and faded out of sight.

It would be the first and last time that Seymour ever saw John Davenport, but this chance meeting and Davenport's instructions would prove to be the most important guidance that he would ever receive. Davenport's timely message had set the stage for the beginning of what would become a supernatural legacy destined to be delivered by none other than Seymour R. Prater.

To get the rest of this story and other books by this author, please visit…
LSYDNEYFISHER.COM

HAVE YOU HEARD ABOUT THIS STORY?

Dear Reader,

If you enjoyed this book, please consider leaving a review. Reviews are valuable to authors, and we appreciate hearing from you!

I hope you will join me again on another supernatural adventure.

Until then,

L. Sydney Fisher

www.ingramcontent.com/pod-product-compliance
Lightning Source LLC
Chambersburg PA
CBHW020534290526
45786CB00002B/879